GAME
SEASON

John Humphreys

GAME SEASON

With recipes by
Angela Humphreys

and paintings by
Rodger McPhail

Quiller

For
Max and Maddie

Text copyright © 2008 John and Angela Humphreys
Illustrations copyright © 2008 Rodger McPhail

First published in the UK in 2008
by Quiller, an imprint of Quiller Publishing Ltd

British Library Cataloguing-in-Publication Data
A catalogue record for this book
is available from the British Library

ISBN 978 1 84689022 2

The right of John and Angela Humphreys to be identified
as authors of this work has been asserted in accordance
with the Copyright, Design and Patent Act 1988

Design by Guy Callaby
Printed in China

Quiller

An imprint of Quiller Publishing Ltd
Wykey House, Wykey, Shrewsbury, SY4 1JA
Tel: 01939 261616 Fax: 01939 261606
E-mail: info@quillerbooks.com
Website: www.countrybooksdirect.com

Contents

Introduction

The pages that follow are a mixed bag of sporting recollections, reflections, recipes and pictures accumulated during three score years and almost ten. There are shooting, stalking and fishing stories gleaned from a lifetime in the field and on the water, influenced by the work of finer writers and meeting and talking to other countrymen, for all sportsmen gather moss as they roll through life. I cannot speak for my two fellow contributors but as my twenty-fourth book this is definitely my own swan-song; everyone is supposed to have one book in them but not twenty-five. Thanks are due to the excellent editors of *Shooting Times*, *The Field* and *Country Life* for their permission for me to seek inspiration from my own material to embellish some of the stories that follow.

This is a book that sits easily on three stools, sporting anecdote and reminiscence, game cookery and some wonderful art. Rodger McPhail is one of the finest wildlife artists in the world and his contribution here shows him at the height of his powers. We are lucky to have him onside. As for the recipes, Angela my dear wife of forty years is an accomplished game cook who for many years wrote cookery columns in *Sporting Gun* and *Shooting Times* while her book *Game Cookery* outstayed its rivals by remaining in print for an unbroken twenty-two years and is still going strong. Game cookery is becoming more popular as chefs and housewives come to appreciate the rich flavours, reasonable price, lack of additives and fat and amazing qualities of the wild game which we shoot and fish. The Countryside Alliance has done a wonderful job of popularising it.

Welcome to an easy ramble though our delectable countryside with rod and gun, cook the end result with tried and tested recipes, marvel at the evocative pictures and, if you are not already a member, welcome to the growing club of hunter-gatherers.

John Humphreys
Bottisham
May 2008

CHAPTER ONE

Pheasant

Fenland Longtail

In far-off days, we humble village folk saw the long-tailed bird as a good dinner and little more. The idea of shooting birds that you might miss was abhorrent to a generation of pot-hunters; cartridges from the village ironmonger at almost sixpence each in the 1950s were not to be wasted. The only sort available were Eley Grand Prix no. 5 shot, known locally as 'Grand Pricks' for we abhorred fancy pronunciation that smacked of the 'foreign'. The thought of blazing away at flying birds was not to be contemplated. The old sexton, whose crazy Belgian hammer gun I borrowed, fixed me with a stern, red-rimmed eye when I enquired of him about making flying shots of which I had read in *Shooting Times*. 'Flyin' shots is for gintlemin and fules – and I ain't neither one o'thim.' The ideal sporting target was not only something that stood still for long enough but something gregarious so that you might get two or three with one shot. Covies of partridge were ideal, rabbits when they gathered round the chicken shed, ducks on a flooded dyke or anything else you might line up to send your deadly 'Grand Pricks' rattling through them.

In time the indigenous and common partridge gave way to the strutting pheasant that loved the weedy fields of those spray-free days. It was large, easy to flush and knock down, fed four careful eaters and was yours for the cost of a Grand Prix. A good man might see a pheasant feeding on a field and bet you good money he could bag it. Spotting the bird pecking on a stubble, the matter of who owned it being irrelevant, he would dismount from his bike and stand staring at it. If the bird paid no attention he would move closer and stand again, possibly moving his hand to catch its eye. In time the pheasant became nervous, decided on discretion and walked unflustered to the dyke, and vanished in the dead nettles and Norfolk reed.

Now our man became a hunting panther and, leaning his bike in the long grass beneath a hedge, he took from its handlebars his rusty hammer gun, slipped in a couple of 'Grand Pricks' and walked directly to the spot where the bird had vanished. Our man knew that the longtail would creep a few yards into the thick cover and then hide until trouble had passed. Holding his gun at the port position our intrepid hunter entered the jungle and mantled about; to 'mantle' meaning to walk with high knee lift and maximum disturbance in dense cover while holding a loaded shotgun, as in, 'Let's all line out and mantle about in the sugar beet.' You will not find the word in the dictionary. If he mantled thoroughly enough he would stumble on the bird and with a thrashing of wings and a wild chortle of alarm it would blunder aloft. Taking deliberate aim at a not impossible target, the shooter had every chance of knocking it sprawling in a puff of feathers. Lacking a retriever he was practised in the art of focussing minutely on the very blade of dead grass behind which the bird fell, fixing his eye unwaveringly on the spot and striding to it. Usually he found it immediately but if he did not he dropped a handkerchief and walked round it in ever increasing circles until the bird was spotted.

On finding his prize he pulled out its tail feathers for it would not do to cycle down the High Street with a set of pheasant feathers sticking out of his jacket. It would not do for all to know his business and his sporting triumph was not to be shared with envious fellow villagers. So he travelled with a large cock pheasant concealed about his person with the air of nonchalant innocence of the empty-handed. Before the sun went down the bird was plucked and oven ready. Not for these folk the luxury of hanging game or the preparation of rich stuffing and piquant sauces: such matters were for magazines and posh folk from 'up Lunnon and suchlike'.

Many a pheasant was done to death in that way but such wicked practice was not confined to the peasantry; it took provenance from the gallant Colonel Peter Hawker. When news was brought to him of a pheasant in his village of Longparish Hampshire – irrespective upon whose land it happened to be – he summoned every man, woman and child on the estate and would not rest until he had the bird surrounded, flushed and shot, for he was by his own account, a fine marksman.

The wild marshes of the old fen always held a stock of wild birds, little creeping marsh pheasants that ran rather than flew, with spurs like game cocks and a natural cunning. These birds had in their veins the blood of their ancestors, imported to those parts by what an old fen slodger described as 'thim owd Roomans'. On a snowy winter's day of the sort we used to get, I was out plodding along the Ouse Washes, gun at the ready, Grand Prix in place and dear old Ajax plodding along. In the thin snow was a set of bird footprints; Robinson Crusoe could not have been more excited. They were pheasant tracks; one of our wild marsh ones had passed that way at a run, but expert at evasion as he was he could not conceal his spoor.

Knowing the bird would not fly unless cornered we set off, Ajax snuffling at the indentations in the thin snow. The bird might leap at any minute so we were both sharp set. We followed it to an osier bed. Ajax dashed ahead – an infuriating habit he had – and I heard the whirr of wings and an indignant 'cock-cocking' as my quarry rose, curled round the willows, being unshootable through the twigs, and skimmed across the marsh to pitch on the far side. On we went, hurrying to the landing spot, picking up the footprints once more and resuming the hunt. Now he took us down three long fields, sometimes the prints became lost or blurred where a little drift had built up on a field edge but we were dogged and knew that given time, the hunter will always overtake the hunted. It would be tedious to describe every twist and turn of that pursuit but we took that bird through another flush from some willows when I thought we had lost him, along a deep dyke and then across it, on and on through a whole livelong morning.

● ● ●

A GOOD MILE FROM WHERE WE HAD STARTED so full of hope and three hours later, we came upon the New Bedford River with a dense stand of Norfolk reed along its margin. The footprints went into the middle of it and did not emerge. Ajax went in and I could hear him crashing about while I stood like a coiled spring, breath hanging on the frosty air, with the hammer on the good barrel cocked. Then came the moment of truth. There were five seconds of silence as I guessed the old dog stood on point and then a violent eruption in the thick. A glorious cock pheasant sprang aloft and flared back over my head to escape. Every feather on its body was bold painted in that crystal air. I had one chance and without thinking or trying too hard the gun flew up, all but innocent of choke the rusty barrel sent the shot true and the bird collapsed and crashed down with awful, complete and exhilarating finality. Seize and cherish the moment as, hearing the shot, Ajax came bustling out of the reeds and headed for the fall. I bellowed to him to stop since, for all his other merits, he was a little hard-mouthed; I did not want his crocodile jaws to sully my trophy. For once in his life he did as bidden and I was able to walk up and lift the great prize still warm to the touch and admire the plumage.

It was a moment to savour, to admire the glowing 'church window' feathers, the long unbroken tail, the eyes demurely closed in death. Of course there was the twinge of regret but also quiet pride at our persistence, at old Ajax sticking to the scent and then the final deadly shot. The bird was not to be stuffed into the postman's bag where its plumage might be sullied and tail broken. This trophy was carried home proudly, no false modesty but swinging from the handlebars for all to see and many were the cries from passers by, 'If you get another one, bring it me....' That bird gave its money's worth. It was paraded before the family and the tale of its capture told and retold. It was hung from a hook in a pantry, its feathers smoothed and photographed with the box camera. A small coloured feather was plucked and glued into my shooting diary along with a verbose account of the adventure. A week later it was plucked with all ceremony and the tail feathers kept as trophies. Then came the day of the feast, a Sunday no less, a graceful compliment denoting the importance of my contribution. Never was there a prouder chap than when slices of white meat with golden skin lay on the plates.

I tell the tale at length to show what pleasure, what delight and what fierce pride may be derived from just one pheasant. In those days of scarcity and modest aspirations we appreciated it well enough, but now...? People thought that if to kill one pheasant gave such joy then to kill ten would give ten times that joy and to shoot a hundred would make it a hundredfold. Did they not know that the delight at a single bird like mine could not be exceeded? In shooting 'more' does not mean 'better'.

Now I go on 'posh' shoots and see many pheasants killed and kill many myself but not one of them gives me a fraction of the delight of that single bird all those years ago. If a shooter deigns to pick up a fallen bird himself, and usually he does not, he tosses it onto a pile of others with scant respect, and with not a glance at the feathers, not a thought about what went in to producing it and with not a hint of the wonderment that Richard Jefferies tried to teach us.

Angels from Devon

High pheasants – some might say 'too high' pheasants – have become the fashion. They told the cherry-nosed Devon keeper that, 'the writing chap from *Shooting Times* was coming for a day at his high birds. He thought for a moment, spat into the ditch with the accuracy of sixty years' practice and observed darkly, 'Chap from Shutun' Toimes eh? We'll spoil his aaaverage.....' His wizened face, wrinkled as a pippin, twisted into a rictus grin of pure malice. The old keeper had a point. Contemplating bracken-clad hills cloaked in patchy thickets of broom and rowan brought on a crick in the neck: birds off the top of that would take some hitting for a man from the flat lands.

Those great sportsmen and gunmakers, who evolved the shotgun to its current state of near perfection, designed a sporting piece to kill birds at a maximum range of forty yards. Patterns were worked out using that yardstick and keepers showed birds at that range and usually closer. A thirty-yard bird was about right for most shots so that he would get some, miss a few and have a good day. Nowadays you turn up in Wales or the West Country, get out your 26-inch barrelled game gun and bag of an ounce of no. 7s and there are curious looks. 'Not shot here before then?', enquires a fellow sportsman. 'You're a bit under-gunned old chap.' The speaker hauls from his car boot a monstrous weapon with 32-inch barrels built like a telegraph pole and from his bag some cartridges made for shooting wild geese on the foreshore. 'This is what you want here,' he says, showing you his ounce and a quarter of no. 4s. The others are similarly armed and what remains of your confidence is whisked away like smoke in a breeze.

You stand at your peg gazing up and ahead, neck aching, eyes squinting at the brow of the hill. Sherpa-figures toil upwards, for beaters hereabouts must be half-man, half-goat. Eventually there is a patter of shots from down the line but you see no birds. Then it is your turn and a speck of dust on the glass rim of the heavens catches your eye. A bird, indubitably, but what sort? Crow? Pigeon? Pheasant or partridge? It draws closer overhead and you see it is a partridge but you have to look more than once to make sure. How in the name of all that's holy are you supposed to hit that? What misbegotten son of a keeper laced with a hatred of his fellow man could present anyone with such a bird, make believe it is a sporting target and expect him to hit it? You feel inadequate with your side-by-side scatter gun loaded with standard game cartridges that work perfectly well everywhere else.

The bird is now overhead, the closest it is ever going to be so you have to make a show, even if it is a token gesture. Swinging aloft your piece you make an enormous lead and fire one hopeful shot. You might as well have spat at it for all the good you do and it sails on unscathed. Thus it is for the next five shots and your confidence is at rock bottom. Then at last you clip one. At that range and with the pattern and velocity all but gone, a fluke pellet catches a pheasant under the chin. It takes an age to fall and hits the ground with a thud that would make jelly of a sober man, and it is a wonder it is not pulverised. There are other odd shots where you hear the flick of a pellet catching on a wing and the bird lurches – as best as you can see at that distance – and glides down in a long, lazy parabola to land miles behind. There are excellent pickers up, out of sight behind and they may or may not gather that bird. Should they do so they will not know it is yours, so will not bring it to lay at your feet for one of those warming moments that oil the wheels of every shooting day.

At the end of the drive you count the empty cases and work out that you have a bird for every fifteen shots. Back home you average three out of five. Thus all day it is only the rare lower bird that you have addressed with confidence unless by then your nerves are too shattered to allow you to make even simple shots. The result is that you have pricked a great many birds at long or excessive range, you have had a miserable day and as the idea of game shooting is to have fun, this one has failed. For a thoroughly sporting day there should be pheasants that the guns can hit with the odd tester to stretch them. A good keeper should use his topography to show thirty-yard birds with the occasional forty yarder and that ought to do for anyone. It is certainly what the conventional shotgun was designed for.

I feel sorrow tinged with slight resentment for those who boast of their mighty guns, enormous cartridges and formidable prowess at extreme range. They degrade the sport I love and they have got the basics of shooting wrong: anyone who feels the compulsion to use the shooting field to prove himself in is a man of hidden sorrows and screaming insecurities.

The Buccaneers of Sutton Bridge

The Sutton Bridge shoot in Lincolnshire is a bleak old place. The iron-grey North Sea hisses across the muds, the hammered pewter ripples of the river Nene roll seawards, a wind as sweet as a razor slices in from the Urals and straight through the most vaunted shooting coat. The land is so flat that on a clear day an imaginative traveller might swear that he could see the curvature of the earth. This strip of coast is the Valhalla of many a fine wildfowler – the likes of Peter Scott, Christopher Dalgety, James Robertson Justice, Arthur Cadman, 'B.B.', Frank Harrison and Kenzie 'The Wild Goose Man' Thorpe left their footprints and spent cartridge cases on the foreshore. The village names, Gedney Drove End, Terrington, Tydd Gote and Holbeach read like a *Where's Where* of fowling quarters made immortal in a thousand articles and shooting books.

Such a hard land bred tough people; it does still. The men who farm those rich, bleak acres are a breed apart: robust, independent and generally unclubbable. The notion that such tough nuts might pool their land to form a harmonious shoot is akin to inviting fifty Bengal tigers to form a co-operative. However, two of them welded together this

disparate group of individuals, a feat of people management of which a London PR firm would be proud. In the old days, in true South Lincolnshire tradition, each tenant poached his own pheasants, often from the seat of his tractor. By the end of October there were few left.

Rather more than five thousand acres of prime farmland now is shot as one unit. The tenants plant cover crops and kill their own vermin; the sporadic legalised poaching ceased for now there was a common cause. The wild game population on that light, dry land flourished so that some farmers complained about too many pheasants pecking the daffodil bulbs and drilled corn. One pleaded with the shoot to thin out the 'pests'. The shoot captain told me, 'We came and had a good shoot but he was on the phone next day; "Yew ain't very good shots, they're all back agin…" ' He was groping for words to convey just how many birds there were. He thought for a moment then said, 'Imagine looking at the sky on a clear, frosty night and seeing a mass of stars. Turn the black sky into blue and that is what those pheasants looked like rising from a field of Brussels sprouts.'

Non-shooting tenants are well looked after with presents of game and given a shoot and a dinner at Christmas. Many of them grow cover crops from which they will never benefit directly. As if this were not enough, the shoot has done wonders for the image of the sport. The money from the sale of game sent the playgroup to Legoland, and once they dispatched an oven-ready pheasant to every pensioner living in Gedney Drove End, a gesture that so moved the local poacher that from that day he waived his rights and never again set foot on the estate. If they could melt the flinty heart of a Lincolnshire poacher the effect of this generosity on the general public was spectacular.

There is no shooting rent for the guns are on their own land. The beaters are willing helpers and the fifteen guns are expected to do their share of serious walking. The costs are virtually nil, the pheasants are all wild for to rear birds would be as irrelevant at Sutton Bridge as a Linda McCartney sausage at the wildfowlers' annual dinner.

• • •

O N A BRIGHT DECEMBER DAY I was picked up at the Bridge Hotel which in its heyday witnessed the roistering of a whole generation of famous longshore gunners. Then it was out to the flat lands where earth and sea bleed into sky until it is hard to distinguish one from another. In the muddy farmyard there assembled a cheerful crew of benevolent pirates. Their faces were as seamed as pippins by the gales of half a century, their hands like shovels scarred and callused from the hefting of ten thousand sacks of potatoes and chopping out miles of sugar beet when they were young. The no-nonsense shoot captain mounted a wobbly pile of pallets in the shed and addressed his crew like Tiberius Gracchus haranguing the mob in ancient Rome. One hen pheasant per drive, no grey partridges, ground game and foxes OK as long as they were safe, pick up cartridge cases – the usual stuff but you knew he meant it. There are no peg numbers but it was a case of 'Jim and Fred come with me, you lot go that way with Alan, Lawrence bring in the flank with three others.'

The cover crop was pointed out, a distant smudge where land mingled with sky, a half-mile yomp on muddy ploughing with no short cut. As we approached we became aware of distant specks converging on the same oasis. We had it in a ring of steel. The word was given to stop and three hundred yards from the cover we ground to a halt, catching breath, feeling the bite of a bitter wind, making sure the gun was loaded and barrels clear. On the horizon a ragged skein of brent geese rose and whirled round before landing on a corn drill. A flock of lapwings, wailing eerily, swooped and tumbled on club wings. The eight beaters lined out and tapped forward.

I have seen many driven pheasants in my time, hurled off Yorkshire hillsides, flushed from Devon mountains, driven off cliffs in Scotland and over tall standing timber in Wales. These birds beat them all. A cock pheasant rose, tail fluttering, climbed vertically for thirty yards, selected a line of escape and angled up and away. It did not level off and by the time it was hurtling downwind over the guns it was to me an unhittable dot in the sky coming straight out of a blazing sun, still making height. This bird was the first of fifty that behaved the same way except that each chose a different line of escape, as only truly wild birds will.

Surely nobody could hit these, but wrong again. These chaps could shoot a bit; a burly shoulder heaved, the gun floated heavenwards, a nubbly finger found the trigger, there came a single shot and an impossibly high bird threw back its head and hurtled down to smack and bounce on the silt far behind. Gosh! I did my best and scrambled down a few but to have one's eye wiped on consecutive birds by the same neighbour does wonders for the humility. I put a single pellet in one and it sailed on and away. Gazing ruefully after it I saw it turn three fields away and come gliding back. It pitched forty yards away where a picker up had it in a flash. Not much credit for that one. In the hand the birds were lean and mean, cruiserweights in training as opposed to the sumo wrestlers which many modern pheasants have become. Then it was a nip of sloe gin and on to the next challenge. At midday a magician produced a meaty stew with bread, cheese, fruitcake and wine in the onion shed and then it was out for more of the same.

The sun eased down and dipped its toes in the Wash, the day was done, another that could not be taken away. At Sutton Bridge they have made a shoot from nothing. All their birds are wild, it is cheap to run, it works wonders for the good name of shooting, it provides recreation for hard-working farmers and funds for local projects, and it would be hard to better the quality of driven game. If the shooting world is to rise above the corporate, two hundred tailless chicken day it will be to places like Sutton Bridge that it will look for the way forward.

Boxing Day Raiders

At the bottom of the marsh lane my eight-acre reserve and mixed shoot known as Hunter's Fen was a mass of brown and gold, a tangle of rose bay willow herb, nettles and Norfolk reed knitted together with dead bindweed as easy to walk through as a badly made doormat.

The family Boxing Day knockabout has become a ritual and is one of the favourite shooting days with the most fun and the smallest bag. Our wild pheasants are frisky at the best of times so son Peter was to slip ahead and block off the usual escape route; as often as not they found another but we had to try and second-guess them. Other son David and I with our Labradors, my China and David's Dipper, along with assorted relations, children and hangers-on were to wade through the jungle towards him. We were still formulating the plan when we heard a thrashing in the tangle and a superb cock pheasant, as gaudy as a Pasha, rose with a chortle of alarm. Peter and I fired as one and it clattered own. The dogs made heavy weather of it in the thick cover but at last Dipper hauled it out. While this was happening a stream of at least thirty pheasants did not hang about but flew out at the far end to safety over the bank. The horse had bolted but we were right to shoot that first one, for a bird in the hand is worth a good lot escaping by the back door.

We plodded on and David shot two that darted back along the river, wild birds waiting until the last minute to take to the wing, sneaking out almost unshootable with the craftiness of years of experience. Those birds might have been direct descendants of those the Romans brought over as table birds two thousand years ago and they made nice water retrieves for Dipper.

I found myself doing the thickest of the cover as usual and was about to point out the fact that the oldest chap was doing the hardest work when there came a cry from Peter, 'Fox! Fox!' and there was Charlie scampering back along and over the bank. Peter's two shots made it flinch but no more than a stray pellet and I rebuked him – I had been after that fox for months, foxes were about to breed, how could he miss at that range – and suchlike moaning. Then commiserations and the relenting: 'Don't worry, we've all done it.' But the lad was a bit quiet. Coming back that way half an hour later, Peter's friend Philippa shrieked, 'Look, there's a dead fox.' It had scuttled out of sight over the bank and died. The conversation now took on a new slant as the pressure shifted.

Later, the beaters went home to get the log fire going and the Boxing Day feast on the table. The whole family had made a show by turning out. Days such as these are the ones to savour in years to come when we are far apart and goodness knows what will have become of us. With six pheasants in the bag, we waited for pigeons to flight to the firs. There were not as many as usual and no wind but we got about a dozen before the light faded, in time for the quackers. I had been feeding both ponds and got the boat ready for a voyage to the island on the frog pond so the shooter could face west. Peter and Philippa paddled away propelled by the weed rake to make the short and wobbly crossing. At last light mallard and gadwall came stuttering in. I left two for David on the carp pond but he missed them both. Peter had several shots but I heard only one heavy splash. They were coming in from the dark sky behind and were very tricky. The bag was three mallard for a dozen shots, not too good.

The bag was half a sack of pigeons, a magpie, a fox, six pheasants, a rabbit, three mallard and two moorhens. It mattered not a jot, for the real magic was being out with people who love each other most, having fun and enjoying being together once a year. Shooting and a handful of wily, wild, marsh pheasants were the bonds that held us close.

Recipes

Pheasant is the best-known game bird and most versatile when it comes to cooking. A roast hen pheasant is a perfect size for two people. A larger cock bird will just about serve four if you add bacon rolls and chipolatas. There is nothing to beat a young roast bird served with redcurrant or cranberry jelly at the beginning of the season. Older birds may be casseroled with good old-fashioned English vegetables or any number of accompaniments and sauces from around the world. Only pluck the birds you wish to cook whole. Otherwise save time by skinning just the breast and legs. Either cut off the whole breast on the bone or remove the two breast fillets. Poach, fry or bake the breast meat in one piece or cut it into thin strips for stir-fries. There is not much meat on the drumsticks but the thighs make excellent stews.

Flodden Pheasant

Serves 2

This recipe is from our son David who lives within a bowshot of Flodden battlefield and is addicted to chilli. His family and friends love this recipe but I have toned down the gravy to suit a more sensitive palate. Jamaican Jerk, which adds spice and fire to a variety of dishes, was once used as a meat preservative. It is ideal for marinades, sprinkling into soups and stews or for rubbing into meat before roasting.

1 hen pheasant
1 lemon, cut in half
2 bay leaves
A few sprigs thyme
Olive oil
Jamaican Jerk seasoning
Black pepper

For the gravy
150 ml (¼ pt) red wine
Chicken stock cube
½ tsp green lazy chilli
1 tbsp Worcestershire sauce
1-2 tsp soft brown sugar
Salt and pepper

Pre-heat the oven to 200°C / 400°F / gas mark 6

Place the lemon halves and herbs in the body cavity. Rub olive oil and Jamaican Jerk seasoning all over the bird. Roast at 200°C/400°F/gas mark 6, breast down, for 40 minutes then turn the breast up for another 15 minutes. Alternatively cook in a roasting bag for just under an hour. Remove the bird from the pan, cover and let it rest for 10 minutes.

Mix the ingredients for the gravy plus the juice squeezed from the lemon in the roasting pan, then reduce. Add extra chilli for a fierier flavour!

Festive Pheasant

Serves 4–6

There are recipes that boast at least half a dozen birds boned and placed inside a goose rather like Russian dolls. Any number and combination will work but this recipe only uses pheasant and partridge layered with spinach and topped with sausage meat mixed with chopped apple and herbs. The stuffing may be any combination of breadcrumbs, herbs, nuts, fruit, mushrooms, bacon or ham.

The resulting joint is easy to carve, may be served hot or cold and makes an attractive alternative to the usual Christmas fare.

1 young pheasant, boned
1 young partridge, boned
450 g/1 lb pork sausage meat
1 dessert apple, peeled cored and chopped
1 tbsp chopped fresh herbs
225 g/8 oz young spinach leaves
Salt and black pepper

Pre-heat the oven to 180°C / 350°F / gas mark 4

Mix together the sausage meat, chopped apple and herbs.

Open the pheasant and sprinkle lightly with salt and black pepper. Cover with half the spinach. Open the partridge, place on top of the pheasant and season lightly. Cover with the rest of the spinach. Spread the sausage meat mixture over the spinach. Pull the edges of the pheasant together, sew up with fine string and shape the meat to resemble the pheasant. Place in a roasting tin, join side down. Butter a sheet of greaseproof paper large enough to cover the top of the bird and cook in a moderate oven for 1½ hours.

Serve hot with the usual seasonal vegetables or cold with salads and fruit chutney.

Filo Pheasant Parcels

Serves 4

The finest mozzarella is made in Italy from buffalo milk. The cheese is moulded into spherical shapes and must be kept in whey. Mozzarella is readily available from supermarkets as is fresh basil, which can be bought all year round either in bunches or growing in a pot.

Breast meat from a brace of young pheasants
225 g (8 oz) mushrooms
8 slices mozzarella cheese
16 fresh basil leaves
16 sheets filo pastry
Olive or rapeseed oil
Salt and black pepper

Pre-heat the oven to 200°C / 400°F / gas mark 6

Fry the mushrooms in some oil until just soft. Slice each breast almost in half along its length. Insert 2 slices of mozzarella, a quarter of the mushrooms, 4 fresh basil leaves, salt and pepper. For each breast brush 4 sheets of filo pastry with oil and arrange at right angles to each other. Place the breast in the centre of the pastry and pull the edges together to make a parcel. Place the parcel on a baking tray, brush with oil and cook in the pre-heated oven for 30 minutes.

Serve the parcels hot or cold.

Fen Pheasant

Serves 4

There is food from every corner of the world on supermarket shelves but it is very satisfying to know that everything on the plate has either been home produced or bought locally. In the Fens we have mountains of apples, plums, onions, red beet, celery, leeks, carrots and potatoes, and as one of the last havens of truly wild pheasants, we Fenmen may truly claim to live off the fat of the land. Each region in our fair country has its own local specialities.

This recipe is for a cock pheasant with a few miles under its belt – save young and tender hen pheasants for roasting.

1 old cock pheasant
2 tbsp oil
1 onion, finely chopped
3 sticks celery, chopped
2 carrots, diced
2 dessert apples, chopped
2 tbsp fresh chopped parsley
1 tsp fresh thyme
1 glass red wine
Game or chicken stock
Salt and pepper

Heat the oil in a flameproof casserole and brown the pheasant all over. Remove it from the casserole. In the same oil, lightly fry the onions, celery, carrots and apples. Place the bird breast down on the vegetables, add 1 tablespoon of the parsley, thyme, salt, pepper, red wine and enough stock to cover the pheasant. Heat to simmering point, cover and cook for 1½ hours or until the pheasant is tender, topping up with more stock if necessary. Remove the pheasant and when cool enough to handle take the meat off the bones. Remove the vegetables with a slotted spoon and purée them in a food processor. Blend the purée with the liquid in the casserole to make a creamy sauce. Return the meat to the casserole and heat through gently. Add the rest of the chopped parsley, adjust the seasoning if necessary. Serve with red cabbage and creamy mashed potatoes.

Cajun Casserole

Serves 4

When preparing several pheasants it is a good idea to freeze the thighs in family-size packs to make what we call 'leg stew'. This will contain whatever is seasonal or happens to be in the larder at the time. There is a huge variety of chilli sauces for sale in the French market in New Orleans with names such as Scorned Woman and Satan's Revenge. The more familiar Tabasco sauce has been made in Louisiana since the middle of the nineteenth century and just a few drops will add a spark to soups and casseroles.

8 pheasant thighs, skinned
Oil for frying
1 red onion, finely chopped
1 garlic clove, crushed
1 tsp ground cumin
1 tsp Cajun seasoning
400 g (14 oz) tin chopped tomatoes
1 tbsp tomato purée
1 small glass red wine
A few drops of Tabasco or similar chilli sauce
Salt and pepper
Chopped parsley to garnish

Heat the oil in a flameproof casserole. Soften the onion in the oil then stir in the garlic, cumin, Cajun seasoning, salt and pepper. Add the pheasant legs and brown on both sides. Stir in the chopped tomatoes, tomato purée, red wine and add Tabasco to taste. Slowly bring to the boil then simmer for an hour or until the meat is tender. Adjust the seasoning, sprinkle with chopped parsley. Serve with rice.

Nutty Pheasant Stir Fry

Serves 4

A quick and easy colourful recipe for the cook in a hurry.

Breast meat from 2 pheasants, cut into thin strips
Oil for frying
1 small onion, finely chopped
225 g (8 oz) courgettes, thinly sliced
110 g (4 oz) mushrooms, sliced
1 red pepper, deseeded and sliced
110 g (4 oz) cashew nuts
1 tbsp soy sauce
1 tbsp lime juice
1 tsp soft brown sugar
Salt and pepper

Heat the oil in a large pan or wok and add the onion, courgettes, mushrooms and red pepper. Stir-fry over a moderate heat for 5 minutes, then add the pheasant and stir-fry for a further 5 minutes. Stir in the nuts, soy sauce, lime juice and sugar, and cook for a further minute. Season with salt and pepper.

Serve at once with noodles.

Indian Pheasant

Serves 6

A version of this recipe has appeared in the *Shooting Times* and is included for a group of Essex beaters who were kind enough to say they had tried it and found it tasty. As the meat is cut into bite-sized pieces this is a good way to use less than perfect pheasant breasts. Just discard any dogged or shot riddled meat. You may spend time grinding spices to make authentic curry pastes but I have used one of the many ready-made varieties available. Add extra paste if you like a fierier flavour.

Breasts of 3–4 young pheasants, skinned and cut into
small chunks
1 tbsp oil
1 medium onion, finely chopped
3 tbsp mild curry paste
400 g (14 oz) tin chopped tomatoes
400 ml (14 fl oz) tin coconut milk
3 tbsp fresh coriander, chopped
Salt and black pepper

Heat the oil in a large frying pan and gently fry the onion and pheasant meat for 5 minutes. Add the curry paste and cook for 2 minutes stirring all the time. Add the tomatoes, coconut milk, 2 tablespoons of coriander, salt and pepper. Stir well and bring to the boil. Cover and simmer for 30 minutes. Taste and adjust the seasoning if necessary and garnish with the rest of the chopped coriander.

Serve with rice and a green salad.

Ginger Minty Pheasant

Serves 4

Another easy recipe for pheasant and a good way to use up any damaged young birds. Cut the breast meat into strips and discard any dogged or badly shot meat.

Breast meat from 2 young pheasants, cut into strips

For the Marinade
2 heaped tsp chopped root ginger
4 cloves garlic, chopped
2 tbsp fresh mint, chopped
2 tbsp olive oil
Juice of 1 lemon
1 tsp sugar

Place the strips of pheasant meat in a shallow dish. Blend the ingredients for the marinade and pour over the meat. Leave to marinate for at least 2 hours. Place the pheasant and marinade in a roasting tin and place under a medium grill for 5 minutes. Turn the meat over and grill for another 5 minutes so that the meat is just beginning to brown.

Serve on a bed of lettuce with spicy potato wedges.

Prior's Pheasant Pâté

Serves 6

Making pâté or a terrine with raw meat can be a bit hit-and-miss unless you fry a little of the mixture first and then adjust the seasoning. This recipe is made with cooked meat so you can get the flavour just as you like it. This is a good way to use a dogged or badly shot bird which might otherwise be wasted.

1 pheasant, skinned
1 onion, chopped
50 g (2oz) mushrooms
2 cloves garlic
Sprig of rosemary and thyme
2 bay leaves
½ tsp grated nutmeg
1 tbsp brandy
Salt and black pepper
25 g (1oz) melted butter

Place the pheasant, onion, mushrooms, garlic, sprigs of rosemary and thyme, and bay leaves in a saucepan. Cover with water, bring to the boil and simmer for an hour or until the meat is tender. Turn off the heat and allow the pheasant to cool in the liquid. Strip the meat from the bones. Remove the onion, mushrooms and garlic cloves from the liquid with a slotted spoon and place in a food processor with the meat. Add nutmeg, brandy, salt and pepper. Blend until the meat is finely chopped. Add a little of the cooking liquid to moisten the mixture if needed and add more spice and seasoning to taste. Pack the pâté into a dish and seal with melted butter. Chill in the fridge.

Garnish with bay leaves, cranberries or black olives and serve with Melba toast or French bread.

CHAPTER TWO

Grouse

Golden Grouse

The red grouse has a special place in the heart of the shooting man and the discerning chef. There are peculiarities that make it especially endearing and place it on a pedestal above the silly pheasant and hedge-hopping partridge of the stubbles. Those may be reared in any number your heart desires but not the grouse. While it is technically possible to rear a grouse, it is a wild bird for which the keeper can do little save protect it from its enemies and manage the heather on which it depends for food and shelter. The red grouse is unique to the British Isles, found nowhere else and that too makes it special. Other countries have their own sub-species but we have the original, the most famous and of course the best. It is the fastest game bird that flies and also the most challenging. Shots who perform well enough at low-ground game find their come-uppance swift and certain when they first address driven 'muir-cock'. He is on you and past before you have mounted the gun.

The first driven bird I saw in North Yorkshire was on a windy day. Standing in a butt, in itself a new and grand experience, peering into the teeth of the gale, the drive was petering out when the beaters flushed an old cock grouse two hundred yards in front. Knowing their reputation for being a bit nippy I addressed it well out of range in front, blotted it out, swung a bit, twitched a bit more and fired. The moment I pressed the trigger that bird was directly over my head and my shot passed twenty yards behind it. I heard the hiss of its wings as it flashed by. As for my second shot, least said soonest mended.

The grouse lives in a few remote places, desolate heather moors far from human habitation, parts of great estates run on feudal lines and difficult for most sportsmen to access. It is an expensive bird to shoot, exclusivity making it attractive to the well-heeled, often from overseas who are especially eager and have the means to pay for large bags. Figures are out of date the moment they appear but there were prices quoted of £150 per brace for driven grouse and a good bag for one day might exceed two hundred brace. As our American pals say, 'Do the math....' Grouse may be, and often are, shot on a shoestring by small farmers with patches of heather or lucky chaps who can drop in on glut years or have sufficient local knowledge to buy a little day of a few brace walked up over dogs. However, grouse are usually shot by the well-off and while today much of the money is 'new' rather than 'old', the bottom line remains the same.

As well as being the finest sporting bird in the world, the red grouse comes with a veil of mystique and magic that the common pheasant will never have. It lives in wild and beautiful places, its guttural 'gobec- gobec- bec- bec- becccc...' sets the pulses racing. It is the first game bird to come into season and the 'Glorious Twelfth' is a date resonant for more people than just shooters. The moors in early autumn are places of stunning beauty, of tumbling streams snaking down gritty rock faces, heathery knolls just crying out for picnics, stony outcrops, steep slopes and mercifully flatter uplands populated by birds rarely seen elsewhere. There are harriers, merlins, golden plover, the eerie wailing of curlews and showers of pipits and larks rising from the heather. Snipe spring from boggy corners, little brown trout live in the burns, sometimes an eagle glides over, high and stately and spoils your shooting, you might spot an adder before it spots you and bumble bees blunder from the pollen-heavy heather tops. No wonder the old-timers longed for 'The Twelfth' to take them north, away from city fumes and the grind of office or corridor of power.

Euston Station in London was the Northern line that took the sportsmen away from town after a hot summer and it presented a fascinating sight on the eve of the season as shooting parties and their retinues gathered. Dogs on leads, smartly dressed keepers, boys carrying leather double-gun cases, rod boxes and cartridge magazines that weighed a ton. Porters wheeled heavy luggage to the guard's van, the air was rich with cigar smoke and the perfumes of Chanel. There were tweeds, Ulster capes, deerstalker hats and above all an air of suppressed excitement for everyone loves to go on holiday. How have the birds done this year? What was the weather going to do? In a few hours the grime and smog of the city streets would be swapped for springy heather and air like champagne. The roar of busy traffic would give way to the wild cries of moorland birds and the crack of a beater's flag. There are many poems written about Euston Station at the start of the season, one of the best being by Maclain Ruadh. It does much to capture the highly charged magic of the occasion and by implication the red grouse that it celebrates.

EUSTON STATION AUGUST 1932

Stranger with the pile of luggage proudly labelled for Portree
How I wish this night in August I were you and you were me!
Think of all that lies before you as the train goes gliding forth
And the lines athwart the sunset lead you swiftly to the North.

Scabious blue and yellow daisy, tender fern beside the train
Rushing Garry, brawling, tumbling glimpsed and lost and seen again
Think of breakfast at Kingussie
Think of high Drumochter Pass
Think of Highland breezes blowing through the heather and the grass.

Lovelier still the moors unfolding
O'er the Slochd you blithely press
'Ceud Mile Faillte', Gaelic greeting
Welcomes you to Inverness.

Change of platform, change of engine
Whistle blast and steaming West
On the stretch of line bewitching
Towards the Islands of the Blest
Achnasheen and Aschnashellach, Achanault and Diurinish
Every moor alive with covies, every pool a'boil with fish
Every well-remembered vista
More enchanting mile by mile
Till the wheeling gulls are screaming round the steamer on the Kyle.
Rods and guncase in the carriage, wise retriever in the van
Go! And good luck travel with you
Wish I'd half your luck my man.

The Numbers Bird

The development of the breech-loading gun first shown at the Great Exhibition of 1851 was a giant leap forward for game shooting which began early in the 1800s with muzzle-loaders and grew in popularity in the second half of the nineteenth century as the quicker-firing guns made in London came on stream.

Possibly the finest game shot in England at a time when the British firmament was peppered with shooting stars was Lord de Grey, Second Marquis of Ripon. In a shooting lifetime he bagged about half a million head of game from rhinoceros to snipe including 241,234 pheasants between 1867 when he was fifteen and his death in 1923 at seventy-one. He met this end in a curiously appropriate way. Shooting driven grouse with his usual skill he killed fifty-one birds in the drive. The whistle blew to mark the end, he handed his gun to the loader, stepped out of his butt, took out a cigar, lit it and fell stone dead in the heather. His only possible regret might have been that it was lunchtime and not the end of the day.

The red grouse was ideal for driving and became the staple early season bird for the 'big shots' and in those days they swarmed. Keepers could be ruthless with anything they deemed vermin, the moors were kept quiet from walkers and other disturbance and those chaps knew how to shoot. A longstanding record was made on 12 August 1915 at a time when there was sterner gun work in the trenches, when eight guns shot 2929 grouse in six drives which, without the subsequent pick-up, yielded 459, 629, 612, 284, 440 and 269 grouse per drive. The same party shot large bags on the following two days so that three days produced an extraordinary 5971 and by the end of October the same beats had produced over fifteen thousand birds. It would be tedious to recount the times when in excess of 2500 grouse were shot in a single day but in the early part of the twentieth century the feat was not uncommon.

We may not leave the world of statistics without mentioning the feat of Lord Walsingham, one of the great shots of Edwardian England who was eventually to be ruined by the cost of his sport and ended his days in penury in Paris along with others like him. It was said that his lordship invited Edward VII to shoot on his moor at Blubberhouses in Yorkshire. His Majesty turned down the invitation but was heard to mutter to a neighbour that he believed that Walsingham had few birds on his ground and sport was likely to be poor. Word of his remark reached Walsingham and, determined to nail the insult, decided to shoot the moor on his own and show what could be done.

The result was a personal bag of 1070 that has gone into the shooting hall of fame or infamy depending on how you regard such feats. He started at 5.12 a.m. and arrived home at 7.30 p.m. He alternated drives up and down the wind and, the moor being hour-glass shaped, was ideal for funnelling the game over a narrow point although Walsingham did not always use the same butt. His best drive produced ninety-three. On the day they picked 1036 but twenty-two were gathered next morning and a further twelve found when shooting the same ground two days later. Some birds were shot on the way onto and off the moor. He fired about 1550 cartridges including forty signal shots not fired at birds. This makes it a phenomenal feat of marksmanship although we might guess that by the end of the day the grouse were exhausted and not keen to fly. Malicious reports were put about that in the afternoon the dogs picked up almost as many as were shot. He killed 1056 in 449 minutes giving him an average of 75 per cent kills per cartridge, assuming you pass over the picked-by-dogs slur.

Writing to a friend a fortnight later Lord Walsingham says,

'Had it been a good breeding season I am afraid to say how many might have fallen: you will say there were quite enough as it was. The one thing everybody says is, "How tired you must have been – how your head and shoulders must have ached", etc etc. I fired 3¼ drs black powder all day and never had the semblance of a headache or bruise of any kind nor was I in the slightest degree tired. I played cards the whole evening as usual.'

There is no record about what HRH thought about it all.

One could compile a book of grouse shooting statistics but it would be a tedious catalogue. A summary would conclude that fine marksmen made some phenomenal bags like Sir Frederick Milbank's 728 in a day, 190 in a single drive: Major the Hon. J. Dawnay almost matched the feat. Once a covey of ten driven grouse were shot by three guns in five shots while Maharajah Duleep Singh, another of the great shots, bagged 440 walked up to his own gun in Perthshire in 1871. Mr William Scott Elliot of Dumfriesshire had an enviable record, dying in his ninety-first year having been out on the moors for seventy-four successive Glorious Twelfths from 1824 to 1898. Many of the bags of the glorious days are unlikely to be repeated and the results of a single drive then, today would be considered a good bag for a whole day.

The last word on statistics appears on a gravestone in Bewcastle, Cumbria commemorating Jonathan Telford of Craggyford, one of the 'moor game shooters of the North of England', who once bagged fifty-nine grouse for seven double shots. That such a feat should be achieved is one thing but to have it recorded on your gravestone as the finest and most memorable act of your life is quite another.

The red grouse lends itself to statistics but my favourite story cocks a snook at the great shots and concerns a simple road mender who could neither read nor write. Breaking stones on the side of a Scottish road he noticed a covey of grouse whizzing towards him, swinging round the contour. Seizing his big hammer he reversed it, raised it like a gun and aimed at the leading bird as it jinked past. 'Bang', he shouted at the crucial moment. Imagine his surprise when his bird collapsed in the air and fell fluttering in the heather where, after a short pursuit, he bagged it and put it in his dinner bag for a broil when he got home. The theory was that the bird had suffered a fractured wing that had healed well enough for it to fly but the effort of jinking when it saw the road mender flourishing his 'gun' was enough to snap it again.

I leave aspirant Great Shots with that thought.

Stonesdale

In North Yorkshire in the Dales, a place of tumbling streams grey lichened rocks, steep slopes and romantic birds there is a grouse moor. It is no Wemmergill or Bowes for there were never many grouse on it and on some days it was a struggle to make four brace, but it was our moor, the link that held together a curious and disparate group of people. I say 'held' rather than 'holds' for it has been taken away after

quarter of a century of fun – the owner decided he wanted it back, as he was perfectly entitled to do – and the fellowship was broken. For fifty weeks of the year the disciples led humdrum lives like everybody else but briefly came alive when they tramped the wild distances. Memory dulls the pain of leg-aching tramping without a shot, facing rain that slants up the hills and into faces and of wearisome slogs that go up and up seemingly forever.

On the plus side – and how much there was on the plus side – there were first grouse, a first driven grouse, the first right and left, the grouse of a son or other loved one, each of them an excuse, as if one were needed, for a celebratory dram or two. We braved the mosquitoes and lay out in the tussocks by the tarn for a mallard, that boggy hole found by following the line of telegraph posts over the hill, the one to which we staggered with buckets of barley to feed and which usually showed a few mallard or teal. We would recall the magpie blur of a rising blackcock, a rare bird for us and in later years we put a moratorium on it but not before the storybook was full of black game stories. Blackcock fly faster then you think. His grey wife was always spared unless it was a case of mistaken identity. The Greyhen of the Year Award was made with due ceremony, once to someone who the night before had been pronouncing about how easy it was to distinguish a greyhen from a grouse.

It was a sad and wild place to the unknowing, a bleak, hostile landscape but we loved it. It was the home of many creatures as well as red and black grouse. Redshank rang their silver bells, snipe drummed like old nanny goats, curlew wept their sad calls, peregrines moustached like pantomime villains arched across the heavens, harriers quartered the ground like setters, short-eared owls, kestrels, merlins, linnets and pipits all lived there along with great brown and green frogs and lizards basking on sun-drenched rocks. Swaledale sheep ran, stopped, stamped and stared with randy yellow eyes before dashing away. There were sheep dogs, lean and mean collies, streaking chips of black and white floating up the hills, so obedient to whistle and shout they put our gundogs in the shade. Wiry shepherds wrested a hard living from this tough place, men hewn from their own limestone, impervious to the weather, wearing battered old coats fastened round the middle with string. We too had our beloved dogs, great soft Labradors, scatty little spaniels and sometimes a fastidious bird dog. They got in the way, ate the scraps, howled at night, bickered, made messes on the verge but we forgave them their faults and each man secretly believed his dog to be the best not only on the moor but in the whole wide world.

• • •

APART FROM THE MOOR the lynchpin that held this odd group together was the cottage that crouched at its foot. Half a millennium old with damp walls five feet thick, once home to a shepherd with rheumatism it had changed little since long dead masons put hand to stone. It was stuffed with sleeping bodies, guns, gunslips, drying boots, coats, bottles, and game bags. It boasted three bedrooms and peaked at hosting forty-one guests each of whom slept more or less comfortably and enjoyed a full English breakfast. After that feast we assembled on the stone patio, the boots were hauled on, the coats checked, the cartridges counted (while you do not expect many shots, should you run out on the high tops it is a heck of a way back for supplies). Then came the briefing that all present could recite, the drawing for position, the lining out at the bottom and the apprehensive glance ahead at the steep slopes to be climbed before even the hope of a shot – the ritual was unchanging. We set off trudging through the cotton grass past sheepfolds that were old when they cut off the head of Charles I, conserving our energy for the hard slog that lay ahead.

At last we reach the tops with a few pauses for a breather on the way; the older we become the more frequent the stoppages. The walk was worth it for the purple plain of heather stretches far away and we hear the guttural shouting of an old cock grouse. 'Go back-back-back...' he cries but we do not heed his advice. Good to know there is at least one out there. The line, grown ragged on the long pull up the hill, is straightened and off we go, wading through the heather, pollen like talcum powder blowing from the flowers, dogs more or less to heel or bustling in the cover ahead.

Just when one foot is deep in a peat hag and the other waving wildly in the air there comes a dry rustle of wings and a covey of eight rises close in front, fleeing round the contour with a throaty chuckle. You mount the gun; blot out the closest bird, swing and fire. Walked-up grouse in August are not the hardest targets so with luck there is a puff of pale feathers running and snagging on the woody heather stalks and your first bird of the season falls, bounces and lies still. Your dog has it in a moment and it is in your hand. Can there be a happier moment? You stroke the richly patterned plumage, admire the feathery feet and marvel that a bird brought down by a couple of tiny pellets can survive a winter in such a hostile place. Success adds bounce to your step, suddenly muscles do not ache as they did before and on the signal the line moves on with other shots from here and there, each followed by a welcome pause as a pick-up is made or a dog given time to work.

So the day passes. We pull up collars at a sudden rainstorm; it passes, the sun comes out and great clouds make shadows on the far hill like the pelt on a pinto pony. We take lunch on the heathery knoll where we have taken it for twenty years and, where a century ago, tweedy Edwardians took theirs. The remains of an old lunch hut stand by as proof that we are not the first to pass happy times here and doubtless we will not be the last. Their lunches might have been more lavish than our cheese sandwich, apple and chocolate bar washed down with a can of ale but at least we carry our own. No ponies tread daintily up the hill with panniers bearing hot soup and lobster salad. Somnolent we sprawl, gazing through half-closed eyes at the horizon, enjoying the privilege of just being there and thinking of many friends who wish they were with us.

Off again, sometimes backtracking, wheeling, covering the ground and every so often a rising covey or an old singleton and spatters of shots until the sun swims down. Rosy-cheeked we head for home, losing the high ground. Those with blisters can really feel them now and unfamiliar muscles cry out. Back at the cottage we fling ourselves down on the warm slabs where eight hours ago we stood so eager for the off. Twenty brace are laid out on the stone wall to be admired, aged, strung into braces and taken into the cool of the cart shed. Those were the hardest earned twenty brace in the world but the most enjoyably procured. After a mighty steak and kidney pie later and a few somethings to drink you seek out your sleeping nook and in about two seconds are snoring with the best of them.

Next morning we disperse, waking to find some early birds already crept away and on the road back home to the real world. In time we join them but as we dice with death on the motorway we see in the mind's eye the blooming heather, the springing covies, the dogs quartering, the joy, jollity, sportsmanship and camaraderie – how all sport with the shotgun ought to be.

Hail and Farewell

That magical place was not ours forever. The ancient stones, the cottage and moor were timeless but not the people who come, strut their little lives then fade and give way to the next generation. We lost our moor where we had such happy times and perhaps it was as well that the blow was swift. When we started we were in our prime, young lions to whom no day was too long, no walk too far. We went up the hills like stags, marched until sunset in the hope of a last-minute covey. Time passed and the buoyant striding lost its bounce and became more of a route march, heads down, facing the rain and eyes down for the treacherous tussock that would send us tumbling. Pauses between walks grew longer; the breathless cry to 'take five' saw us collapsing into the heather like pole-axed steers. Although the morning starts grew later and the walk off in the evening grew earlier, curiously the bags grew heavier – no point in getting old unless you grow crafty. Then the thought stole into the backs of minds, 'If I shoot this bird I will have to carry it for the next six hours.' Sad when a shooting man reaches such a parlous state.

In quarter of a century there was no weather and no adventure we had not witnessed: heatwaves and tempests, driven snow in August, rain that drove up sleeves and into flared nostrils, flat calm and a sun that blazed down with tropical heat. As for tests of marksmanship: we shot grouse crossing, going away, curling over the line, driven, flaring out at the sides, rising singly and in covies twenty strong. We shot young, old and middle-aged birds, in storm, flat calm and placid sunshine. We painted the cottage and in a flush of energy hauled sets of enormous lorry pallets up the hill to make into butts. We did more driving and less walking as age crept up on us adding a new dimension as long as we could muster enough friends, children and family to beat.

Our children were conceived and born, if not actually in the cottage, during our time of friendship. First young mothers carried them up the hill in papooses, then they tottered along as junior beaters and in time, when they were about ten years old, they came to shoot a grouse. A list of those who shot their first on our moor would fill the parish register. Each one was faithfully recorded in the leather-bound game book that immortalised our adventures.

Dogs from field trial champions to the useless and hopeless, the hard-mouthed, the runners-in, the unruly and the bad tempered came as puppies, then did their best, grew old and grizzled, faded and died. Some lie buried beneath the heather where they were happy.

The parties in the cottage became legendary. There was discordant singing, impromptu jazz bands and wild congas wove an unsteady path up the hill at two o'clock in the morning. These events led by pillars of the community! We went home on Sunday and on Monday the dustbin men came to the deserted three-bedroom cottage in the middle of nowhere and gazed in wonderment at bags and boxes overflowing with empty bottles.

The wild grouse were the golden thread that bound us all together but, as in most human affairs, it was the people who were the bones of the place. On that moor we grew up, formed friendships that last to this day, some of us died, others married, children were born and one by one we dropped out as the hills grew too steep and limbs lost their elasticity. It was a poignant moment when an old friend standing on the top, almost unable to catch his breath, grey-faced with exhaustion, knowing that he had made it to the top for the last time, gazed on that scene with tears in his eyes. Yes, we were on the wane.

A new landlord tolerated us for a few years and then without warning chucked us off. The magical land of frogs, pipits and the red and black grouse was lost to us, the fellowship was broken and we went our separate ways. We did other things in August like gardening, visiting the supermarket and what 'normal' people do but there was an ache in many hearts. The hills remained implacable, unchanged by our passing; a finger placed in a river and then removed, that was us. No sign left save some home-made, wooden butts already succumbing to the savage winter weather to show where we had been. In time they too would be gone.

We may not have left an impression on the moor but what it did for that disparate group of human beings was incalculable. It taught us much about sportsmanship, tolerance, handling bad conditions, shooting, wild birds, making and maintaining friendships and the developing and nurturing of a generous spirit. It taught us more perhaps than one might have learned in the humdrum intercourse of the workplace. What that moor gave us was inestimable, and the people and the memories are indelible.

A dead grouse hanging by a string is much the same wherever you find it but the circumstances in which it is bagged are what make it special.

Recipes

Grouse feed mainly on heather and berries and have a unique flavour, stronger than other game birds. Bad weather and disease mean grouse are often in short supply and therefore highly prized and expensive to buy. Treat them as you would any game bird and select only the young for roasting: about 30–35 minutes in a hot oven is about right. Grouse are by nature leaner than partridge or pheasant so it is a good idea to wrap the birds with rashers of streaky bacon or pork fat. This will help to keep them moist without masking the flavour. Traditional accompaniments are bread sauce, breadcrumbs fried in butter and gravy. Allow a bird per person. Older birds need longer cooking and by adding extra ingredients a brace of birds can feed four people.

Grouse Veronique

Serves 2

This is an easy recipe suitable for any young game bird. The grouse is sautéed with shallots and mushrooms, then gently poached in white wine and crème fraîche with a hint of tarragon. Green grapes are added to the sauce giving this French dish its name.

Brace of young grouse
1 tbsp olive oil
2 shallots, finely sliced
110 g (4 oz) mushrooms, sliced
150 ml (¼ pint) white wine
2 tbsp crème fraîche
1 tsp tarragon leaves
Salt and black pepper
110 g (4 oz) green seedless grapes

Cut each grouse in half with sharp scissors or game shears and trim away the backbone. Heat the oil in a large frying pan and soften the shallots and mushrooms. Add the grouse halves and sauté over a medium heat for about 10 minutes until the meat is cooked, turning 2 or 3 times. Transfer the grouse, shallots and mushrooms to a flameproof casserole. Add the wine to the frying pan, deglaze and bring to the boil. Turn the heat down and stir in the crème fraîche, tarragon, salt and pepper. Add the wine sauce to the casserole, cover and simmer for 5 minutes. Add the grapes to the casserole and heat for a further 2 minutes.

Barbecue Grouse

Serves 2

Grouse are in season just as the elderberries are ripening. As well as wine and cordial the berries make a strong flavoured jelly which is a perfect accompaniment for grouse and venison. As long as they are young, game birds are delicious cooked outdoors on a barbecue and make a welcome change from sausages and burgers. Cranberry or redcurrant jelly may be used instead of elderberry.

Brace of young grouse
4 rashers streaky bacon
4 dsp elderberry jelly
4 sprigs thyme
Black pepper

Cut each bird in half and remove any remaining innards. Season with black pepper and wrap a rasher of bacon round each half bird. Lay each half bird on a square of foil and top with a dessertspoon of elderberry jelly and a sprig of thyme. Close the foil parcel making sure it is well sealed. Cook for 20 minutes on a hot barbecue.

Greenlaw Grouse

Serves 2

This is a quick and easy recipe, equally good with duck and pigeon requiring just the breast meat. Use the leg meat for pâté or stock. Rowan and hawthorn are complementary flavours for all game. Wood from the rowan was thought to have mystical powers and it was often used as a supporting beam over the fireplace and for making plough handles to bring luck to the farmer and ward off evil spirits. Thanks go to Marjory for a supply of her delicious rowanberry jelly.

Breast meat from a brace of young grouse
1 tbsp oil
4 tbsp port
1 tbsp rowanberry jelly
1 tbsp crème fraîche
Salt and pepper

Heat the oil in a frying pan, add the grouse breasts and cook for 3 minutes on each side. Transfer to a plate and keep warm. Add the port, jelly, crème fraîche and seasoning to the pan, stir well to blend the ingredients and heat through. Spoon the sauce over the meat and serve at once.

Tan Hill Grouse

Serves 4

This famous pub, the highest in England is a watering hole for grouse shooters and ramblers walking the Pennine Way. The local brew goes well with veteran grouse with a few moorland miles under their belts. No extra vegetables are needed except some creamy mashed potatoes to soak up the gravy.

Brace of mature grouse
Oil for frying
110 g (4 oz) bacon, chopped
1 onion, chopped
2 large carrots, diced
2 large parsnips, diced
110 g (4 oz) mushrooms, chopped
300 ml (½ pt) Theakston's Old Peculier (or similar strong ale)
300 ml (½ pt) stock
3 or 4 sprigs of thyme
1 tbsp elderberry or hawthorn jelly
Salt and black pepper

Cut the grouse in halves and remove any remaining innards. Heat the oil in a large flameproof casserole and brown the birds and bacon. Add the chopped vegetables, ale, stock, thyme and seasoning. Bring to the boil, cover and simmer for 1½–2 hours or until the meat is tender. Check the seasoning before serving.

Clay Pot Grouse

Serves 2

A clay pot is similar to the earthenware cooking vessels used by the Romans. They are large enough to take a cock pheasant or a brace of partridge or grouse. This is an ideal way of cooking birds of doubtful age. The meat stays moist, retains its flavour and does not need basting. The pot must be soaked in cold water for about 30 minutes, so that it can absorb the moisture, and then placed in a cold oven.

Brace of mature grouse
150 ml (¼ pt) orange juice
1 large orange, sliced
Sprigs of rosemary
1 tbsp elderberry or cranberry jelly
Salt and pepper

Soak the pot for 30 minutes in cold water. Stuff a slice of orange and a sprig of rosemary inside each bird and truss with string. Place the birds in the pot and add 2 tablespoons of the orange juice. Put on the lid and place on the lowest shelf of the oven. Set the temperature for 200°C/400°F/gas mark 6 and cook for 1½ hours. Put the rest of the orange juice and the fruit jelly in a small saucepan. Add the juices from the pot and heat to dissolve the jelly. Add salt and pepper to taste.

Garnish the birds with orange slices and sprigs of rosemary. Serve the gravy separately.

CHAPTER THREE

Partridge

The Prince of the Stubbles

Many of a certain age cut their shooting teeth on the partridge, either the dear old greys or the immigrant redlegs, nicknamed 'Frenchmen' by a Victorian duke because he claimed, 'They run from the guns.' In days long gone it was the common game bird before the silly pheasant took over. Back then foxes were rare. Every parish had keepers who eliminated anything that might be an enemy of game, and farms were unsprayed patchworks of small fields, rough dykes and hedges. This was partridge heaven and it produced heavy bags in the golden age when Six Mile Bottom vied with Elveden who competed with Holkham to see which could amass the biggest pile of the slain.

Tradition was to walk up the birds over a kite flown by a boy; this had the effect of making them sit tight fearing that the kite was their old enemy the hawk. I started in the post-kite era but before driven bird shooting found favour in the rough, weedy fields of the old fen. Every September it was out on the Hercules bike, the sexton's hammer gun with the dodgy second barrel suspended between handlebars and seat pillar, and a rangy yellow Labrador name of Ajax at heel – I was into Greek heroes rather than foaming sink cleansers at the time. At ground-eating pace, the dog loping by the rear wheel, we eased down the slope onto the wild old fen, levelling out for a mile or so until we came to the dilapidated farmyard of my friend, Stanley Robinson. Hens scratched, pigs squealed, piles of sacks lay in the barn, chaff swirled in the wind and rusty farm machinery that Turnip Townsend would have recognised stood in the nettles. There was rarely anyone there. Hiding the bike under a slouching straw stack, off we went with a postman's bag flapping emptily, the gun loaded with two Eley Grand Prix no. 5 cartridges, and Ajax pottering about roughly but by no means always in range.

The technique was simple enough. You quartered the fields because at that time of year the birds would sit tight. Back and forth from ridge to ridge of the potatoes or through the weedy sugar beet we strode throughout a hot September day, nose reddening, legs beginning to tingle until, when least expected, there was a whirr of wings, a reedy chirrup and you had walked right into a covey. Pick a bird, take your time, for at 12/6 (about 65p) per box cartridges were not to be wasted. Fire a careful shot, change to a second and hope that the unpredictable barrel behaved itself and, with amazing luck, you might have a brace in the bag, assuming Ajax did his stuff.

Then it might be a hare, up and streaking through the dry potato haulms, maybe a mallard flushed from a wet dyke, every shot carefully taken and no risks; minor sales of game helping to pay for ammo. As the sun swam down and a harvest moon rose, it was back to the farmyard where we had started so long before; legs weary, dog panting and the bag, that flapped so emptily now cutting into the shoulder. Finally we toiled up the endless slope into the village and home for a proud exhibiting of the bag and bangers and mash with father's runner beans for supper.

The pride was doubled when it came to the dinner at which my own birds were the star turn: post-war austerity meant that any contribution to the family larder was keenly appreciated. Unfortunately my mother was not a good game cook, wartime rations and

making do she could manage but more exotic fare was too much for her. She was of the belief common in those days that everything should be 'boiled to buggery' as my uncle remarked. The dish of my partridges was born in triumph to the table, the lid removed and there lay a row of what looked like brown, varnished cricket balls and about as tender. Father jabbed his fork into the nearest one. The tines bounced off the leathery hide and it skittered across the table, skated on the polished surface and landed in the lap of my aunt. Father said that we might as well have one each and do our best with it; after all we all had good teeth.

Spanish Cannonballs

I stand as still as a war memorial, staring crook-necked at an angle of 45 degrees, gun held lightly by the wrist, stock on hip, a coiled spring ready to pop. Sunglasses reduce but do not eliminate the glare of a semi-tropical sun. Cotton trousers, short sleeved shirt and floppy hat are a welcome change from the stuffy, Victorian tweeds of old England. The view that commands my full attention is an arid, steep and rocky hillside dotted with aromatic sage and rosemary bushes. The hill is dusty, khaki brown, as brown as only a hill can be in sunny central Spain. A great bird swings and wheels over the bluff, arcing round on stiff wings. Julian, the Spaniard at my side, grunts and spits: '*Aquila*' he mutters. The black shadow floating over the sun-drenched earth might cause the birds either to squat or leak out of the drives down secret gullies. He tilts and glides out of sight round the bluff. Julian holds my second gun, a brace of cartridges jammed between stubby fingers. His ragged moustache twitches, he too stares in silence at the rim of the distant hill, both of us as nervy as two recruits looking out over No Man's Land before a big push.

Somewhere in the sun-baked heart of La Mancha, an hour from Madrid lay the Hundred Valleys estate run by English gamekeepers on English lines. This could pass for a traditional covert shoot or an ancient partridge manor with its maize and kale strips, although there are giveaways that tell you it is not. One is the weather, a cobalt sky and sun in winter; another is the lunch tent pitched in the hills, a gilded, be-flagged pavilion

45

that belonged to an Indian Maharajah at the time of the Mutiny; or it might be the *tapas* that confront you at every turn. Pause between drives and, as if by magic, there is a snowy tablecloth and basket chairs beneath a shady tree. As the echo of the last shots rolls and fades in the hills, attentive staff spring like mushrooms from the earth inviting you to the driest of sherries and biscuits with anchovies, olives and local cheese. That is definitely not the British countryside in mid-winter.

The wait is over; there is a black speck far and high, buzzing like a rogue bee in our direction. Another shows behind it, then a little cluster like so many Spitfires in formation, fast and purposeful. This is what we came for, despite unease at shooting in front of an audience. A small knot of spectators stands attentively by the olives – they are tough and well-informed critics. Moment of truth, heart pumping, must make a good start, pick the first bird soaring past, fast and straight, get the feet right, find the line, swing through and fire one shot. The bird carries on but from a thing of wings and blurred movement it has become a round ball, only its forward momentum keeping it airborne. Suddenly it sails down in a graceful arc to thud into and bounce in the sage bushes. A squirt of white feathers like smoke from a stricken bomber drifts and trickles.

Antonio my *secretario* makes a cross on his card. One down and the butterflies disperse. There is a gentle nudge, it is Julian my loader or *cargadoro* reminding me to change guns. We do so smoothly and straight away the next squadron of Spanish partridge is upon us, breaking wild this time. Some spew out to left, some right and one of two with immortal blood in their veins climbing and sailing overhead as high as church steeples. Driven partridges look pretty damn quick and so they are, but a yard slower than pheasants. Bigger birds like bigger yachts travel faster than small ones. We get a right and left, Julian is not a man to show emotion but he forgets himself enough to croak, '*Ole; Doublo!*' Praise indeed but I fail to repeat the feat and from the next pair drop only one that wobbles down forty yards to the side. The X-marks-the-spots on the *secretario's* card are mounting up.

My lucky start has got the audience off my back so I can relax and take hits and misses as they come. First impressions have been made and why should we care what others think of our shooting? A poor run leaves me with bruised fingers. My composed pair of AYA no. 1s were the only side-by-sides in the field that day, my five companions sported over-and-unders. Hasty gun mounting meant battered fingers and missed birds so time to take a firm grip and a deep breath; shoot an easy one to restore confidence and work back up to the good stuff. My trusty attendants make little distinction between a good bird and a bad one. All they really want is a heap of the slain for wagers are made

46

as to which 'gentleman' can shoot the most. Hard cash rides on the outcome. Miss too many and you snatch the bread from their children's mouths.

Perma sunshine means there is no rush to get in another drive, 'before we lose the light'. On our two days back to back, we managed five drives one day and four the next. The other statistics are soon told. Six guns bagged a handful short of five hundred per day. The sky was speckled with birds, any one of which would beat out of sight the best you will see in East Anglia. Standing in the valley for the second drive, suitably stiffened by a *fino*, I squinted up at more brown hills tufted with squat bushes, at my side the ever present Julian, burly with horn-rim cheaters. His English was as thin as my Spanish, a shake of the head at a bad miss, a murmured '*bueno*', once or twice an '*Ole*' but his gun changing was as slick as a mouse. My two guns worked well enough in the heat of battle and between us we accounted for our share. Only once in hundreds of changes did we tap barrels lightly, no damage done.

Behind us on a tussock sat Antonio noting the fall of birds so as to gather them later. He had the old-fashioned game counter like a rifle target on which he recorded where each bird fell. His English too was limited, so communication was reduced to him showing me the click counter at the end of a drive so I might know the score. It was no more than a fleeting glance for he had to scuttle off with Julian to retrieve the birds. Voices are raised should a neighbouring man presume to pick up someone else's bird.

Another wait, the citrus taste of anticipation on the tongue and then a trickle that became a flow of partridges buzzed over. The sky was a sheet of blue paper on which someone had shaken a pepper grinder. Bang-bang, change, bang-bang, change shoulder getting sore, overconfident again and beginning to miss; careless gun mounting – a run of misses – take more time – a run of hits – then a really high one, '*Ole!*' – then two moderate ones feebly missed. The wind had risen making the birds curl wickedly, shots rattled up and down the line and still the show went on, it seemed forever. Could there possibly be another partridge left in Spain? Indeed there could. At last the beaters' flags fluttered on the crest like an advancing army, a few late risers from the facing slope, the final horn, and another drive was over. Pour out the two unfired shells, Julian stuffs guns in slips and stumps off to help Antonio. I peep at his clicker, forty-six for the drive; not so bad for an old buffer especially with high, tricky birds. *Bueno!* Stroll over to the tapas.

To sit at ease on the last afternoon as the sun sinks, sipping champagne in agreeable company, gazing down the long, parched valley while partridges chirrup near and far and your cheeks redden in the sun is to count your blessings. Pinch yourself to make sure you are not dreaming and start to count the days before you can return.

Feeling Blue about the Grey

Faint calling partridges afar,
My son, in briefest words,
The roots beyond the stubbles
Are fair choc-a block with birds.

Patrick Chalmers

Touch as lightly as thistledown on the subject of the grey or English partridge and old-timers in battered tweeds will wipe a tear from a rheumy eye. The grey bird is an icon, a cornerstone in the history of game shooting in these islands, a symbol of great times past, of a kinder, gentler way of countryside management and a rhythm of farm life set by the plodding footsteps of cart horses and the swish of a scythe. When Turnip Townsend and Jethro Tull were tramping the sod, our farming landscape was a chessboard of small fields, wide hedges, long stubbles, acres of turnips and brown weeds. An army of gamekeepers saw to it that every predator, real or imagined, was hung out to dry on the keeper's gibbet and there were no sprays nor brutal, mass agribusiness that sees modern stubbles ploughed in before the combine has left the field. In the old landscape the grey partridge flourished and every field held several covies: walk abroad and showers of brown birds would rise and whirr away like copper pennies shot from a gun.

This was the perfect sporting bird rivalled only by the red grouse. A grey partridge was a wonderful parent, stout defender of its brood, dogged incubator in wet weather and a cunning leader in flight – 'a lion's heart in a sparrow's body' as Fred, the old keeper, remarked. A covey had the glorious habit of flying over a hedge, seeing the guns and bursting like a star shell to all quarters. Fine shots learned their trade on the grey bird a century ago when the East Anglian firmament was full of shooting stars. Walsingham, Duleep Singh, Stoner, Edward VII, Ripon – the great names still resonate. These were shots who could, with double guns and nifty loaders, take four birds each out of the same covey. Great estates whose names became emblazoned in the hall of fame vied one with another and prided themselves on bags running into four figures: Holkham, Elveden, Six Mile Bottom and Sandringham were among them. Like the ill-fated passenger pigeon that blackened American skies and in a decade became extinct, who might guess that the grey partridge would suffer a similar fate?

Smoking cheroots, wearing bold tweeds, Inverness capes and deerstalkers, leather gaiters shining like conkers, their ladies bedecked and bejewelled as pashas, the big shots strolled to their pegs. Under the stern eye of martinet keepers, beaters in smocks carrying flags moved the birds from stubbles to roots and then, in a series of deft manoeuvres, over the guns behind the quickthorn hedge. A cunning flick of a flag and they curled and crackled over, fast-flying, strong on the wing – testing targets for the new-fangled breech-loading guns. Acrid black powder smoke hung in the hollows as shots volleyed, pickers up with dogs quartered the ground behind and a horse-drawn game cart stood patiently in the shadow of the elms. Lunch was taken in a silken pavilion, wine flowed, gloved waiters served rich viands and the aroma of Turkish cigarettes mingled with Floris perfume.

They are long gone, those elegant ladies and gentlemen, the chatter of their conversation whispers eerily along quiet coverts. They have passed and taken the grey partridge with them, a bird they believed to be as perennial as the grass. Modern farming killed it as did over-protection of raptors, changing weather patterns, the explosion of the fox population, deadly sprays that stole the birds' insect food, fewer keepers, short stubbles and uprooted hedges – vandalism subsidised by the government.

To lose such a bird would be the saddest indictment of countryside management, so before it sank into oblivion a ray of hope appeared in the form of The Game Conservancy Trust (GCT) that adopted the bird as its emblem. They persuaded politicians to put right some of the damage, replace hedges, outlaw toxic sprays and pay farmers to manage land in a more friendly way. The grey bird became the barometer

of the environmental health of a farm. In October 1952 the late Sir Joseph Nickerson made a record bag at Rothwell by good management, fine gamekeeping and a run of dry summers. GCT research showed us what the bird needed and in isolated pockets, notably Her Majesty the Queen's Sandringham Estate in Norfolk, by expert management, the grey is back in numbers that Lord Ripon might have recognised. Land at Royston in Hertfordshire also has been expertly keepered under sponsorship of the GCT and here too the English bird thrives.

Although the jury is out on the long-term fate of this doyen of sporting birds, it is still possible for a favoured few to walk with ancient sportsmen, to stand as did they in front of a hedge red-peppered with the wild fruits of autumn on a golden September day, to hear from afar the chirruping and wait with pounding heart for the first covey to burst over and test their mettle. Manage to knock down a brace and at that moment you walk in the footsteps of giants, and a patter of ghostly applause laced with cigar smoke wafts on the breeze from somewhere behind the oaks.

Border Bombshells

To show redlegs well you need a gale or undulating ground or both. The weather is down to luck but if you release birds in low hills you will have quality sport. Doug Virtue discovered this in his vastness in the Lammermuir Hills in the Borders and here he shows wonderful partridges. Get a wind up there on a shooting day and you have birds to die for.

On drive one we stood in a narrow valley, more a gully really and stared up at the crest where strips of bracken and gorse glowed russet. We basked in sunshine at a time when rainstorms deluged the rest of the United Kingdom, a rare treat for the bleak Border country. Beaters were at risk of growing one leg longer than the other for they crabbed along a precipitous slope; at almost every step a squirt of birds rose, spread like a fan and arrowed across the valley. Gosh, they were testing but the old rednecks in the team struck lucky for they all came onto form at once. Shots spattered and rolled, partridges one moment urgent and fast, shrank and spun tumbling down to thud into

the short grass on the slope behind. Shooting was continuous and there were more than enough birds for you to get your eye in. We gathered at the end with bright eyes, each with a tale to tell of amazing hits or inexplicable misses. We boasted of rights and lefts, of eyes wiped and confessions of the odd low bird taken in the heat of the moment – in other words the same chitchat as you find on any good shoot. The drive produced seventy birds.

The secret ingredient of this shoot is not only the ideal terrain but also the swathes of bracken and gorse that cloak the hills. There are no cover crops but strong and healthy birds live *au naturel* in small coveys on the slopes. They behave and fly like wild partridges and this gives them a stunning edge as sporting quarry. It also produces a wide variety of shots. While many birds are steeple-high sailing over at extreme range, some bank and sweep round the contours like driven grouse, and many will not cross the valley but curl and skim along the face of the hill in front. This means that on any one drive the gun is presented with every shot in the book but the number of birds shown is such that he can be picky.

The beaters emerged from the gorse, a team of pickers up homed in from behind and between them they gave the ground an efficient hoovering. Many of the guns had dogs and they helped. Very little was lost. Too many shoots hurry on to the next drive without picking up carefully. It was a short stroll along tussocky grass and an about face, and we were ready for the second drive. But surely Doug had given us his best one first and subsequent ones would not match it? Not a bit of it. If anything the second drive was more prolific than the first. Again the redlegs shovelled over from every angle, many of them very tall, others coming in small coveys round the bluff, zipping down the wind at hideous speed. Again gun barrels grew hot and we realised that, had we been able to afford it, we could have used double guns. A quick head count showed that already we had exceeded our limit but we decided to take lunch then and have one more drive in the afternoon, hoping that our respective bank managers would be understanding.

We went for lunch at the Thistle Inn said to serve some of the best Aberdeen Angus steaks in Scotland. Doug explained that his birds come from wild, local stock and over twenty-one seasons he has been upgrading, and improving the bloodlines by selective breeding, and culling anything less than perfect. The parents are fed on unmedicated rations, which means a high degree of disease immunity in their progeny. The result is a hardy, healthy stock of robust, well-feathered birds that produce returns well above the national average. Doug added,

'We can show high flying, sporting birds capable of beating the very best guns. Another bonus is that at the end of the season we are left with surviving hen pheasants with strong wild bird characteristics which, properly keepered, are capable of rearing young in the wild. This provides a generous stock of home grown birds produced naturally.'

Back on parade the sun had faded and a light drizzle set in. We faced another range of rocky outcrops, more bracken and whins where I noticed that tracks had been cut to allow beaters to get through. We did our best, hit some and missed some. The three keepers in matching tweeds, who double as game farm workers out of season, worked their dogs picking droppers. My little Labrador, China, was into the prickles and brought back five birds all alive and ignored the dead ones. She really was a star. The tally was mounting when two pickers up hove into sight with bulging bags.

The final count was 254 brilliant redlegs for three drives and eight guns. Days of such superb and consistent quality do not come along often and when they do they are to be savoured.

● ● ●

Up to high Norfolk a week later for a few more but after The Lammermuirs, no Norfolk partridge held terrors. Drive one I stood in a field of carrots, one gun out from the high hedge, gazing along it to a strip of maize and sorghum behind it. A single bird came at me high and dead straight overhead. Oh no. Once a favourite shot this is now one to dread. No time for the Stanbury shuffle to turn it into a high crosser so I gave it my best effort and it sailed on unscathed, no doubt to the critical acclaim of my fellow guns. Then some easier ones to right and left, every one missed in style. I felt like a tennis player armed with a cricket bat up against Federer.

The final hooter couldn't come soon enough so I took China to help my more accurate neighbours pick up, for carrots are bad for scent. Blessings on the picker up who came up with a partridge saying it was my first bird, which I thought I had missed, that came wobbling down and fell at his feet. May that man prosper and his wife bear many sons. Things could not get worse and, as often happens, they got better. Next drive we got a few fair ones and then stood behind a tall thorn hedge facing a stiffening wind.

The birds came wonderfully, one here, one there, a right and left and a snappy one that should have been missed. Then came a singleton, a little dot hurtling over high as the steeple of Norwich cathedral. Starting well in front and keeping swinging I loosed off. It turned into a little feathered cricket ball and in a graceful parabola sailed down to earth miles behind. One to be proud of and we finished the drive with a dozen.

By the time of the last drive confidence was high. We were sufficiently relaxed to pick blackberries from a hedge. Lips stained with juice we limbered up at the sound of the whistle and were ready. The hedge peppered with all the fruits of autumn in the colours of a pop artist's palette bewitched the eye. Two birds fell out of the first covey to curl over, the next three were missed clean. That was the end of it and the shooting gods had done what they do so often and so well, cast you down, raise you up and leave you with nagging doubts. Doncha just love it?

Recipes

Partridge have a delicate flavour and young birds are best plainly roasted in a hot oven. Traditional accompaniments are game chips and bread sauce. Older birds are better casseroled for a longer time at a lower temperature. They may be cooked in stock, wine or cider with a variety of vegetables or fruit such as mushrooms, shallots, tomatoes or apples. Allow one young bird per person – this may be cut in half after cooking to make it easier to manage. An older bird may be halved to serve two if casseroled with plenty of vegetables.

Plain English

Serves 2

As they are virtually fat free partridge need to be kept moist during cooking. One way is to wrap the birds in streaky bacon or buttered greaseproof paper. I prefer to use a self-basting tin or cook in a roasting bag with a little flour, salt and pepper. There is no need to baste the birds as they cook in their own juices and stay moist and succulent. The meat browns through the bag and the oven stays clean. This works equally well with grouse and pheasant.

Brace of young English partridge
1 tsp flour
Salt and pepper
Crab apple or elderberry jelly

Pre-heat the oven to 180°C/350°F/gas mark 4

Open out the bag and add a good shake of salt and pepper and a heaped teaspoon of flour. Shake to coat the inside of the bag. Place the birds in the bag and turn to coat them with the seasoned flour. Seal the bag loosely with the plastic tag. Place in a roasting tin and with scissors make a few slits in the bag. Cook in the preheated oven for 35 minutes. Slit open the bag, remove the birds and keep them warm. Use the juices from the bag to make a thin gravy flavoured with a little crab apple or elderberry jelly.

Partridge with Parsnip and Pepper Sauce

Serves 4

Parsnips are one of our more versatile root vegetables. They enhance winter casseroles and are excellent roasted alongside potatoes or a joint of meat. Alternatively, cook chip-size parsnips for 5 minutes in boiling water. Drain and dry the parsnips then brown in olive oil. Turn off the heat and stir in enough honey to coat the parsnips and, for a crunchy texture, add some sesame seeds. Also, an equal quantity of parsnips and potatoes make a mash with a difference. Liquidised, parsnips thicken sauces and make tasty soup. In this recipe a dash of hot pepper sauce and a pinch of nutmeg spices up the sweetness of parsnip without overpowering the delicate gamey flavour of the partridge.

Brace of old partridge
450 g/1 lb parsnips, peeled and quartered
Clove garlic, chopped
Hot pepper sauce
¼ tsp nutmeg
450 ml (¾ pt) stock
Salt and pepper
Knob of butter
Thyme leaves
Sprigs of thyme to garnish

Pre-heat the oven to 150°C/300°F/gas mark 4

Cut the birds in half, remove any remaining innards and trim the backbone. Place in a casserole dish and add the parsnips, garlic, a dash of hot pepper sauce, nutmeg, salt and pepper. Pour over the stock, which should just cover the partridge and parsnips. Cover and cook in the oven for 1½ hours or until the meat is tender. Remove the birds and arrange on a serving dish. Cover and keep hot while making the sauce.

Purée the parsnips with a knob of butter in a blender or food processor. Place the purée in a saucepan, stir in the cooking liquid and bring to the boil. Adjust the seasoning if necessary. Pour the sauce over the partridge, sprinkle with thyme leaves and garnish with sprigs of thyme.

Spanish Partridge

Serves 2

As well as memories of impossibly high birds while in sunny Spain with Sally and Michael Cannon, there are also memories of a landscape dotted with vineyards and olive groves, the heady perfume of wild herbs, dry sherry, olives, tapas and toasted almonds between drives. With no rush to beat the fading daylight to squeeze in the afternoon drives, lunch was a leisurely affair with more tapas followed by barbecued meats or partridge cooked in the local Spanish style. Fortunately the ingredients for one such recipe are available in this country – though I cannot guarantee the sunshine!

Brace of partridge
Olive oil for frying
1 large Spanish onion, finely chopped
2 cloves garlic, crushed
450 g (1 lb) tomatoes, skinned and chopped
1 tbsp fresh rosemary and thyme, chopped
White wine
12 black olives
Salt and black pepper
Sprigs of rosemary or thyme for garnish

Select a flameproof casserole just large enough to hold the partridges. Heat the oil in the casserole and brown the birds. Remove from the casserole. Soften the onion in the oil, add the crushed garlic, chopped tomatoes, herbs, salt and pepper.

Place the birds breast side down on the vegetables and pour over enough wine to cover them. Simmer gently for ¾ hour or until just tender – make this nearer 1½ hours if using mature birds. Add the olives and cook for a further ¼ hour.

Garnish with fresh herbs before serving.

Red Hot Partridge

Serves 4

Mrs Beeton wrote, 'Partridge should be chosen young, if old they are valueless.' Today the bag is likely to contain more red than grey partridge and a few of these will be old but should not be wasted for, with imaginative cooking, they are well worth eating and far from valueless.

Brace of mature redlegs
Oil for frying
1 red onion, chopped
1 red pepper, deseeded and chopped
1 tbsp tomato purée
2 cloves garlic, crushed
2 tsp chopped fresh red chilli or 'lazy chilli'
Salt and pepper
450 ml (¾ pt) stock
420 g (15 oz) tin red kidney beans in chilli sauce
400 g (14 oz) tin chopped tomatoes

Pre-heat the oven to 170°C/325°F/gas mark 3

Cut the partridge in half with sharp scissors or game shears and remove any remaining innards. Heat the oil in a flameproof casserole and brown the birds. Remove the partridge then soften the onion and red pepper in the casserole. Add the tomato purée, garlic, red chilli, salt and pepper and slowly add the stock. Stir in the tin of chopped tomatoes and return the partridge to the casserole. Cover and cook in a moderate oven for 1 hour. Add the red kidney beans in chilli sauce and cook for a further ½ hour. Check the seasoning and add more chilli if you like it really hot.

Partridge in a Pear Tree

Serves 4

If you want a change from turkey and all the time-consuming trimmings why not save any grey partridges you get during the season for a special Christmas lunch? This can be prepared in less than an hour giving the cook more time to spend opening her presents.

4 young grey partridge
Zest and juice of a lemon
4 Conference pears
150 ml (¼ pt) red wine
150 ml (¼ pt) water
1 tsp soft brown sugar
½ tsp ground cinnamon
4 whole cloves
4 tbsp single cream
Salt and pepper
Watercress

Pre-heat the oven to 190°C/375°F/gas mark 5

Place the zest and juice of a lemon in a saucepan. Put a quarter of the lemon shell inside each partridge. Secure the legs to the parson's nose and place in a self-basting roasting tin. Cover and cook in a hot oven for 35 minutes.

Peel the pears whole leaving the stalks on. Place in the saucepan with the lemon zest and juice. Add the wine, water, sugar and spices and poach for 10 minutes. Remove from the pan with a slotted spoon and keep warm with the cooked partridges. Strain the poaching liquid into the roasting pan and de-glaze. Stir in the cream and heat very gently. Add salt and pepper to taste.

Arrange the watercress on the plates to form the tree, then add a partridge and a pear. Hand the sauce separately. Serve with roast potatoes, Brussels sprouts with chestnuts and spiced red cabbage to add colour to this festive meal.

CHAPTER FOUR

Wildfowl

The Black Isle Geese

I t lacked an hour to dawn. The cold did more than hold, it gripped with the icy teeth of a frozen vice. Donald the keeper's eyes and nose were a matching mauve and shivers vibrated through his tweeds. At the sight of the hip flask his rheumy eye grew animated. He had an awesome reputation and had been known to drain one in a single swig; it was rumoured that when a metal flask was applied to his lips, the suction was so powerful that the sides met in the middle. My companion Arthur Cadman took the first pull before passing on the precious liquid. Fastidiously Donald wiped the neck of the flask on his sleeve and took a ferocious swig. Being glass rather than metal the sides did not meet and it was extricated from his grasp while there was still some left.

There was a symphony of goose music on the loch in front. The overture was a guzzling chatter punctuated with the high-pitched yelp of an old gander telling his fellow Vikings that the eastern sky was about to lighten. Then it would be time for the singing, shouting battalion to thunder inland to the 'tatty bottoms' for breakfast. Arthur's magnum, a serviceable weapon that could tell a tale or two was propped against a whin. I had my 8-bore, not everyone's first choice, but old reactionaries would rather shoot one goose with the old girl than ten with an ordinary gun. An 8-bore and a pinkfooted goose are made for each other. That gun which had shot geese in three centuries lay on a game bag on an earthen bank, her great horn hammers on half cock, 'loaded for bear' with two and a quarter ounces of 3s in each barrel.

The eastern sky paled to apple green with dainty streaks of pink, the wind rose from the shore, it would be in the birds' beaks when they flighted and might bring them a few feet lower. Now we could distinguish objects: the rowan tree with a kestrel sitting atop, the derelict drystone wall and the grubby barley stubble in front falling away to a single-strand barbed wire fence festooned with sheep's wool. Pheasants cock-cocked and grey partridges creaked; Donald twitched into life, 'Geese, geese,' he hissed, 'geddoon quick.' Sure enough a small group of great birds had risen far off and with the light behind them beat straight towards us. The eight was seized, thumb on a hammer and face buried in the grass but, by twisting the neck, half an eye was cocked to the heavens. They came closer and we could hear a delicate hooting. They were whooper swans. Donald muttered an apology; 'Easy to be mistaken in this light,' he mumbled. Five minutes later came another lot just the same; 'Dinna worry, it's just more swans, they always flight first.' This time we stayed put and watched them approach; seeing our faces they veered and there came a guzzling 'ank-ank' of alarm. It was a small skein of greylags. This time Donald could think of no excuse. What goose guide calls swans as geese and geese as swans with successive lots? I cancelled his next go at the flask.

No mistaking the next lot for the gabbling that had risen to a crescendo fell silent as at the throwing of a switch. Then with a roar like the flying Scotsman passing a wayside halt they were up and every voice burst out clamouring, singing, shouting their wild battle cries and a fierce paean to the dawn. The sound and sight never fails to stir and there they were, a muddy thumbprint on the oil painting of the dawn, two thousand geese up and spreading out into chevrons, echelons and every formation known to heraldry. Arthur is an old hand and hardly moving seemed to shrink into invisibility like a hare dropping into a form or a cock pheasant on an open corn drill when it thinks it has been spotted: now you see it, now you don't. Mittens felt clammy on hands and the rolled-up balaclava itchy on the forehead, slipping slightly over the eyes; no time to adjust it, the geese might spot the movement. The first skein was overhead but no twitch of movement from the master, too high, but on my own I might have chanced a whack at them. There is nothing like experience and Arthur allowed the first waves to pass unsaluted. Then came what he was waiting for, the tail end Charlies, the hangers-back that fly lower than the leaders.

They came in a shallow vee, about a dozen of them and even with a magic wand a magician could not have placed them more directly over our heads. Respectfully we waited for the great man to shoot first. The legendary Kenzie Thorpe used to instruct his guns, 'Nobody shoots until I shoot.' Ever tried to shoot second-hand, flaring geese? Arthur bided his time and rose to address a young goose at the end. Another thing you learn with the years is never to shoot the leaders if you intend to eat them. The old fork-benders tend to be in front, the rear gunners are goslings of the year, excellent with rich gravy. At his shot the bird hunched and staggered, half recovered, and leaving nothing to chance, he gave it the second barrel, another mark of the old hand for geese have amazing powers of recovery. My two shots failed to touch a feather. There was the healthy boom of black powder, gout of sparks, acrid whiff of smoke and a sheet of flame followed by a not ungentle double heave on the shoulder but nothing fell. There was the sound of a rattle of pellets on wings but Arthur said it was only the echo of the explosion reverberating from those great radar scanner pinions.

Arthur always had good fowling dogs, he wrote a book about them. None would have won a trial nor caught the eye on a covert shoot but for wildfowling they were wise, hardy, bold and above all, bag fillers. The dog of the moment was a raw-boned, independent beast named Sam and he set off unbidden to look for the goose that had fallen down the hill in a field of kale. Seeking to redeem himself for earlier indiscretions Donald lurched off also, tripping in the whins and snagging his breeks on the barbed wire. He could have saved himself the trouble for Sam was already on his way back with the dead bird clamped in its jaws, one great wing trailing in the mud, eyes demurely closed in death. Donald panted back and eyed my hip flask pocket as does a terrier a bug. 'Guid shot sorr,' he proclaimed.

Many geese now were in the air, the pale sky seamed with black dots. Donald blotted his copybook again by calling a pair of barnacles that skimmed round from behind intending to land on the stubble. The gun was up and swinging through before we spotted the magpie black and white, and pulled out just in time. Donald knew exactly what the birds were and that they were protected but wanted us to have a shot at them anyway. The flight was all but over when Arthur shot a wonderful right and left from a skein passing to his right, both birds dead and both retrieved. The 8-bore too finished on a high note for just when it seemed that every goose had flown, a tight knit lot came straight overhead, a chance for redemption after the earlier disaster. The third bird down the line was the one and at the 'pwoooomph' it carried on unscathed but the two behind it came tumbling down, a whirling of wings and flailing necks. The second shot was dispatched blindly into the brown and to my gratification and surprise another goose at the back threw up a wing and plummeted to thwack into the muddy stubble. It was up and running like a redshank trailing a wing but Donald spurted after it and threw himself bodily upon it for Sam was busy with other retrieves.

Such mornings are for the special page in the shooting diary, to be recalled in tranquillity and gloated over while memory lasts. We had six geese, three each, and had seen a morning flight to stir the soul at a time when most people were in bed. Six pinks lay in a neat row on the sheep-nibbled sward, their feathers stroked, wings arranged neatly for us to admire. The three down to the 8-bore were all flukes but no less valuable for that. Back in the village the pub would be open and waiting for, in The Black Isle as in the rest of Scotland, they never close. I knew too that there would be a large platter with my name on it, heaped with a breakfast for which a hungry fowler would do anything save folk dancing...

By now Donald had become a model of quiet efficiency. He carried the birds, helped us over fences and held our guns enthusing about our wonderful shooting. He was a dear old rascal, now, along with Arthur Cadman and Sam, long gathered to the great game larder, so who could begrudge him the final draining of the hip flask? He sucked so effectively that he drained it, no drop remaining. His face wore a beatific smile as he held open the door of the car. A crumpled note sank into a callused palm: 'I'll be bidding ye good day,' he said and turning on his heel faded and vanished in a stand of silver birch by the roadside on his way to his wee cottage and breakfast.

As the only one of that expedition still above the sod, I come over all misty-eyed when I recall it. Tame pheasants have their place but wild geese and an 8-bore in Scotland? What would a shooting world be without that marriage made in heaven?

Teal Trouble

A half gale ripped across the lone and level acres of the wide fen. Tawny tasselled reeds thrashed and bent double as though trying to break loose from their moorings and fly away. The wind shrieked through shock-headed willows guarding the droves like dwarfish sentinels. Water on the sword-straight dykes and drains was tossed and turbulent. There were times when the little van veered dangerously across the road, not so good in those parts where roads are bounded not by reassuring, impact-breaking hedges but by deep waterways that can swallow a motorist and his vehicle in a blink. It might be a week before they find him. In times of frost, snow or wind, locals drive with caution in the middle of the road.

Only a madman or a wildfowler would be out on such a day and the destination was a bend in a remote fenland river where nobody went save the odd pike angler or botanist. The van eased into its berth beside the collapsed bale stack, bales that spoke of a golden harvest long gone as the straw was now bleached and mouldy. Then it was the plod on the flood bank, bag flapping emptily on back, the old BSA magnum tucked under the arm and a sweet natured black Labrador named Drake wandering vaguely nearby. Walking at heel was not one of his conspicuous strengths, finding birds and filling the bag were more in his line. We crabbed down the lee of the bank seeking shelter, passing drains full of eels and thick brown reed beds through which the wind hissed like a bag of fenny snakes.

After the best part of a mile we came to the old spot where a lagoon had formed on the river wash, a sheet of shallow open water over bottomless mud. A string of mallard rose quacking hoarsely and beat into the wind; climbing, banking round and forming a shallow vee they toiled away westwards, crabbing across the gale. It would not do to wander carelessly into the water for the mud would suck you down and you would never be seen again. In summer shoals of red-finned rudd dimpled the surface picking up flies. The lagoon was connected to the main river by a narrow channel through which the fish swam and departed the same way. Once an otter slipped sinuously across the surface, caught our scent, whistled a warning and slid beneath the surface. They are the most graceful animals and in those days were a rare sight.

The reeds round the pond were on shifting sands, ground that trembled and shook like jelly at footfall. The intrepid fowler walked on a thin crust of rotten reed beneath which was the bottomless mud; it would not do to break through. Six mallard decoys bobbed on the water, anchored to the bank with willow pegs. The hide was simple, a few Norfolk reeds bent over to make a little bower, but with the wind so strong, building was next to impossible and sitting still or kneeling on my canvas bag might have to do. Drake would lie down with a wisp of dead rush draped over him. He was used to hiding and keeping still.

The pageant of the evening unfolded. A string of wild, fen pheasants flew low across the wash and settled, some in thick reeds and some on the flood bank where they would roost or 'jug' as we called it. Cold-eyed gulls flew in tight formation high overhead making their way to the distant sea. Showers of finches and tits scuttled in the reeds and a lone cormorant beat heavily downstream, his day's fishing done. Then there were new birds in the air, more purposeful and clean cut than the cormorant or even the gulls. They were teal, beating into the teeth of the wind, flaring, flying low across the river seeking the shelter of the lagoon.

I dropped my head to my chest peering under hat brim, crouching stock still keeping the giveaway flashes of human skin out of sight. As is the way with teal they flared suddenly, cut round and swirled past in front – this was the moment. The old BSA flew to the shoulder, the barrels sought out the leader swung smoothly and the shot was on its way followed immediately by the second. Three teal at the front suddenly shrunken and aimless turned into tennis balls that crumpled and fell lightly onto the water. As is their way the survivors flared heavenwards, rocketing up showing why springing teal is a testing shot. Three down for two shots was a good start and now it was Drake's turn to earn his biscuits. He was out of the hide and tripping lightly across the lagoon, keeping moving to prevent getting stuck. He would have been hard to rescue but he was an old hand and retrieved two birds at once, a trick he had, one head hanging one side, the other opposite it from that black velvet bag he called a mouth. 'Get back!' He went for the third, not so easy, for this one had struggled to the shore and hidden in the reeds. After two minutes galumphing about there came the triumphant plunge followed by snuffling breathing that showed that he had something in his mouth – the third teal.

It was too good to last, for teal test even the best shots of which the writer is far from one; they have razor sharp reactions, they flare more quickly than a pigeon at the flash of a white human face, and when the first shot misses the second is hard to get off as they burst away like supercharged grey partridges. The next five chances were missed for the wind was stiffening. The stalling incomer is a hard shot, easy to 'poke' and miss behind for it seems not to be moving although of course it is. What was more, the heavy three-inch magnum was not the right gun for the job, far too cumbersome, more fitted for geese on the foreshore than teal dropping into a puddle on a fresh marsh. A light game gun, a 20 bore or even a 28 would have been ideal.

Now the birds were coming in rushes and this was shaping up to be a flight of a lifetime. You shoot well if you relax and so I started to 'throw' the gun, swinging more casually, not trying quite so hard. The result was a run of hits, some first barrel kills and second barrel misses but not so bad for teal. A small gang of mallard came chattering round on the same line, hanging in the air looking for a sheltered spot to land. After the teal they were fish in a barrel and two of them splashed down heavily before the survivors were whisked away on the storm to find a safer berth for the night. Then a bonus, a mothy flicker wafted downwind from the direction of the flood bank. This was no teal and it took a nano-second to recognise the blunt shape and long bill of a woodcock, flying out to feed in the gloaming, as they do. No time to aim or make any calculations, it was a purely instinctive shot, a rise, swing and squeeze. By luck the 'cock balled and fell into the brown tangle of water docks on the river's edge. Drake worked on it for three or four minutes but he had watched it fall. Then he was galumphing back with it in his mouth, a proud moment.

● ● ●

T HE TEAL THEME RETURNED, more fell and old Drake was not out of the starting blocks as quickly as earlier. He was beginning to feel his age but the timing was right, it was almost too dark to shoot and the flight was drying up. Birds approached and dropped silently onto the water before they could be spotted. The backdrop of the flood bank now was too dark to pick them up before they landed. A goodly pile lay in the trampled rushes along with the confused browns of the woodcock and the bottle green of the drake mallard's head. Such bags are not made every day and it might be a while before another flight like that happened along. Thirty-six teal were counted into the old postman's bag plus three others, a fair weight to lug along the lonely flood bank, keeping a weather eye open for Black Shuck, Old Meg and other ill-natured fenland ghosts.

Drake plodded behind, his earlier bounce gone and we were a tired couple who found the old van parked where we had left her in the lee of the old stack. A rub with a rough towel to dry the old dog and settle him on his warm sacking underneath the car heater, a blessing for wildfowlers and their dogs. Every one of those little ducks was to be eaten, an evening on the plucking machine showed them as fat as miniature farmyard geese and they would be full of flavour. The teal was traditionally the ladies' duck being of small size although ladies these days have healthier appetites and aspire to mallard.

One must be careful with shooting a heavy bag of a wild, non-replenishable bird and most fowlers stop short of killing more than for their immediate needs. However, just once or twice in a lifetime there comes a flight when it is all right to fill your boots.

Canadian Sunrise

Old fowlers are almost as good at yarn spinning as old fishermen. One of the myths they try to perpetuate is how delicious roast wild goose tastes. This is not true for they carry little fat, one more than a year old is tough. The old joke about boiling a brick with the bird and when the brick is tender throw away the goose and eat the brick is apposite. This is only partly true, for a good cook can make a wild goose eat well enough for fowler's fare but you might not put it on the table when the bishop comes to dine. The recipes in this chapter are as good as any and have been tried and tested. As for hanging, you can hang it virtually forever in cold weather. One old fowler went into print with his suggestion to hang an old greylag for at least a month in frosty weather with an onion stuffed into its body cavity.

The goose that breaks the mould is the introduced, feral Canada goose. It was brought in as an ornament for, despite its size and strength, no wild one could cross the Atlantic. The Canada is not popular for it breeds too successfully. Aggressive and territorial in spring it bullies lesser waterfowl so that no mallard dare nest nearby. It likes to graze greensward with a preference for fresh corn and the choicest golf courses where its overactive bowels plaster the sward with guano to the despair of the sportsmen. Most farm crops are to their liking and, because of the damage they do, it is permitted to shoot them out of season. For all that it is also a sporting bird, highly prized by American waterfowlers, indubitably a goose and therefore fair quarry. It is easy to miss, sharp-eyed and best of all the geese on the table, especially if you get a young one. They eat only the best fresh food and do not often frequent the tide, tainting the flavour. The secret in all goose shooting is to aim for the birds near the back of a skein and not the leaders. Those in the van are likely to be of great age and incredible toughness, 'fork bucklers' they used to call them, whereas those at the rear are the birds of the year, tender and innocent.

There was a gaggle feeding on old stubble deep in the heart of the lonely fen. You could see them every morning sitting like dumpy teapots, standing, walking about and plucking at spilled grain and sprouted greenery. Pause awhile and glass the peewits, golden plover and flocks of chattering starlings feeding among the very feet of the great birds, so close that sometimes they were hissed at. The geese flew in every morning from the reserve beyond the high flood bank that kept out the waters of the lode, a drainage

and communication channel dug by the Romans that bounded the field. In its day that waterway saw some exotic traffic passing by. If ever a place lent itself to an ambush this was it.

Scanning the field it was obvious that the place to hide would be close to the foot of the bank where a straggly line of rusty barbed wire ran along the boundary. The geese would beat in low over the bank within easy range and too late to change direction by the time they recognised the danger. The larder was light of a good Canada so the bag would not be wasted. Before first light I tramped along the dew-soaked stubble, wearing waders and a soft brown coat for comfort and protection for the dawn had a raw edge. Behind, there slouched a grey muzzled old Labrador, Kenzie by name, who knew more about goose shooting than many humans; a fowler could wish for no finer companion. Finding a spot that lined up with the middle of where the gaggle of yesterday had been feeding, two oxblood red cartridges slipped into the breech, the magnum clunked shut and was leaned on the fence. Five mallard skimmed round and settled for the grain which was thickly spilled. A wet harvest meant that the combine had missed almost as much as it gathered so birds and beasts flocked to the feast. Hares lolloped and rabbits scuttled on the far boundary. Twittering softly flocks of small birds landed like a shower of sparks from a grindstone. Somewhere a covey of grey partridges called creakily and redlegs shouted in answer, 'chuck ooor... chuck ooor...'. A cock pheasant wandered on the far side until he saw us watching then dashed into the safety of the bankside willows.

It was almost broad daylight and surely time for the geese to flight but from them there came not a sound. I picked up the magnum, one of Mr Rosson of Norwich's workmanlike pieces, not 'Best' London but a sound weapon engraved with a feeding goose on one lock plate and some flying ducks on the other. Wiping the dew off its old English silver finish it was swung experimentally, the breech snapped open to make sure it was still loaded. Alone it is tempting to break some of the safety rules and prop a loaded gun in a handy bush ready for action, a thing you might not do in company. One old fowler would load his gun every time he walked out of his back door to where his bicycle waited to take him down to the sea wall. Once when young he was walking off the marsh with an unloaded gun and a skein of geese appeared head high out of the fog and took him by surprise. That day he vowed never again would he be caught out with an unloaded gun.

Then came the magical sound to set the pulses racing, the wild cry of the geese that has moved fowlers since the days of bows, arrows, throwing sticks and slingshot. Not quite the magic of the grey geese but geese nonetheless and still with the power to stir. l gripped the gun with iron grasp, took a deep breath, dropped to one knee and buried the white human face in the dead brown grass that fringed the wire. In the corner of my

eye appeared a dense black line, barely rising above the top of the bank, doing no more than the minimum to make it to the feeding field. Trouble was they passed sixty yards to the left and so were out of shot. In an agony of frustration they passed, my thumb on the safety catch ready for the next lot. The following skein and the one after followed exactly the same line. They banked into the gentle breeze and angled down to settle on the field, furling their great wings and staring suspiciously about them. Stock still I peeped from under my hat brim until they relaxed and walked about, guzzling the rich grain.

Big decision. Would it be wise to move and get under what was obviously the main flight line or stick it out and hope for the best? On the point of gathering up bag and dog to shuffle along the fence, the decision was made. From in front came a soft croak and there they were, dead overhead, barely twenty yards up, a skein of about a dozen beating steady as a constellation above me. On autopilot it was a smooth rise to the feet, swing of the muzzle remembering the rule to keep away from the old skein leader and fire the first shot. One goose shrunken and aimless cartwheeled down to thump mightily into the stubble. Not the hardest shot admittedly but even easy geese can be easy to miss. The second shot followed the first and a second bird threw back its neck and that too whacked down; had it hit me on the head it would have been curtains. At my shots the feeding gaggles rose with a great clamour, swung round and for a moment there was a chance of a shot at them, but seeing me standing there they veered. Even Canadas are not stupid.

Old Kenzie needed no urging but set off towards one of the fallen birds while I went for the other. We chose wisely for mine was stone dead and his was playing possum, lying neck outstretched but with plenty of go in it. As the dog approached it rose and set off running but the old chap put on a spurt, closed the gap, there was a brief wrestling match and it was safe in his mouth. Getting a good balance he brought it back looking pleased with himself.

There were still geese to come and no doubt the bag could have been heavier but enough's a'plenty. Two would do. Each one tipped the scales at almost fifteen pounds so they took some carrying down that long narrow field to where the old van nestled by the barn. Despite the weight there was a spring in the step and the thought of how good it is when a plan comes together. On the way back there was a stand of newly sprung field mushrooms, that strange fruit of the half-light so good for a fowler's breakfast. They were not there on my way up. I picked a goodly pile and having no extra bag was presented with a pretty problem of logistics on how to get them and two large geese safely home. Amazing what you can do with a red spotted handkerchief and a piece of binder string...

Recipes

Wild Duck

The most commonly eaten wild duck are mallard, wigeon and teal. Unlike the farmed varieties, the amount of fat on wild duck will vary. In September mallard that have feasted on corn from stubble fields may have a good flavour but are thin so are much better later in the winter when they have put on a layer of fat. It is a good idea to roast them on a rack so excess fat may be poured off during cooking. Cook uncovered so the skin can crisp.

Roast mallard for about an hour; a really plump duck may take a little longer though this is a matter of taste. Roast the smaller wigeon for about 45 minutes and teal for 20–30 minutes. Reduce the time if you prefer pink meat.

Apart from the duck you wish to roast which should be feathered in full, just pluck the breast and legs. Pan-fried duck breasts are delicious but must not be overcooked or they will be tough. Breast meat may be sliced before cooking to use in stir-fries or added to salads. Use the leg meat and liver for pâté.

Although duck and orange are perfect partners there are so many other fruits, herbs and spices which complement this richly flavoured meat.

A brace of mallard and wigeon will serve four people but allow one teal per person.

Teal for Two

Serves 2

The tiny teal is often referred to as a lady's duck, it has a delicate flavour and is just the right size for one so may be cooked to individual taste.

Brace of teal
1 lime
Olive oil
1 tbsp clear honey
1 glass white wine
Salt and black pepper

Pre-heat the oven to 200°C / 400°F / gas mark 6

Place half a lime inside each teal, rub olive oil all over the birds and sprinkle with black pepper. Place breast side down in a small roasting tin and cook for 10–15 minutes. Turn the birds over, spread honey on each breast and cook for a further 10 minutes. Remove the lime halves from the ducks and squeeze the juice into the pan. Add the white wine, salt, pepper and a little more honey if necessary to make thin gravy. Allow the birds to rest for 5 minutes before serving.

Green Ginger Mallard

Serves 4

Ginger has been a popular spice in English kitchens since it arrived with the Romans. The spice is derived from the knobbly rhizome of the plant which should be peeled and grated or cut into fine strips. Wrapped in cling film fresh ginger will keep in the fridge or freezer.

Brace of mallard
Bunch of sage leaves
Olive oil
4 tsp ground ginger
2 Bramley cooking apples, peeled, cored and chopped
2 tbsp green ginger wine
1 tbsp clear honey
25 g (1 oz) fresh ginger, finely chopped or grated
Black pepper

Pre-heat the oven to 200°C / 400°F / gas mark 6

For a crispy skin pour boiling water over the ducks a couple of hours before you are ready to cook them then pat them dry with kitchen paper. Place the sage leaves inside the body cavity. Brush the duck with a little olive oil and sprinkle over the ground ginger and black pepper. Place on a wire rack in a roasting tin and cook for 1 hour. Reduce to 40 minutes if you prefer the meat pink. Let the duck rest in a warm oven for 5 minutes.

Place the apples and green ginger wine in a saucepan, cover and cook gently for 10 minutes or until the apple is soft then stir in the honey. Purée in a food processor or beat with a fork until smooth. Stir the fresh, grated ginger into the sauce before serving.

Duck Breast with Cranberry Sauce

Serves 4

Balsamic vinegar has been produced from the Trebbiano grape in the fertile Modena area of Northern Italy for centuries and, unlike most vinegars, it is dark, sweet tasting and can be very expensive according to its age which may be twenty-five years or more.

4 wild duck breasts
2 tbsp olive oil
4 tbsp cranberries
2 tbsp balsamic vinegar
2 tbsp soft brown sugar
½ tsp mixed spice
Salt and black pepper

Heat the oil in a frying pan. Add the duck breasts and cook for 4–5 minutes on each side pressing down firmly to prevent curling. Remove the meat from the pan and allow it to rest in a warm oven. Add the cranberries, balsamic vinegar, brown sugar, mixed spice, salt and pepper to the pan and cook very gently until the berries soften. Slice each breast lengthways and arrange on a serving dish. The meat should be pink and juicy inside. Spoon the sauce over the meat.

Devilled Duck Livers

Serves 4

Duck livers, especially mallard and teal, make excellent smooth pâté. Fry them in butter with a little onion and garlic, then whiz in a food processor with a little melted butter or stock, a splash of brandy, salt and pepper. They may also be added to a game pie or simply fried in butter and served on toast for breakfast. You may need to freeze the uncooked livers until you have enough for a recipe. Be sure to remove the gall bladder before freezing and use within 3–4 months. Here the livers are marinated in a devilled sauce before frying, then served on a bed of mixed salad leaves for a light lunch or as a starter for a more formal meal.

8 duck livers washed and dried
25 g (1 oz) butter
Mixed salad leaves
Basil for garnish

For the Marinade
2 tbsp mushroom ketchup
1 tbsp Worcestershire sauce
1 tbsp soy sauce
1 tbsp English mustard
Dash of Tabasco sauce
Salt and pepper

Mix together the ingredients for the marinade, pour over the livers and leave for 2 hours. Drain the livers and keep the marinade. Melt the butter in a frying pan and cook the livers for 2 minutes on each side. Remove from the pan and keep hot. Add the marinade to the pan, stir and heat through for 1 minute. Check the seasoning.

Slice the livers and arrange them on a bed of salad leaves, drizzle the sauce over the meat and garnish with basil.

Wild Goose

Wild geese may not be offered for sale so most people will only ever taste farmyard birds. Wildfowlers have the opportunity to shoot and eat grey geese or Canadas. Of the grey geese the pinkfoot, whitefront and greylag are smaller than the Canada which is better flavoured than the grey. Only pluck the whole bird if it is young and to be roasted. Otherwise save time by skinning the whole breast and cutting off the meat from either side of the breastbone. Wild goose meat is darker in colour and almost lacking in fat compared to the domestic variety, which has paler but richer flavoured meat and a substantial amount of fat under the skin. A whole roast goose is enough for four servings.

Michaelmas Goose

Serves 4

Years ago pasturing rights allowed villagers to graze a number of geese on common land. These would be sold at Michaelmas goose fairs to raise the money to pay for the next quarter's rent due on St Michael's day, the twenty-ninth of September. This was also the day when landlords held their annual rent audit and traditionally provided a sumptuous feast for their tenants. This was likely to include roast domestic goose.

This recipe for wild goose is adapted from a fourteenth century dish for reared birds using local autumn fruits: apples, pears and the quince, which is an orchard tree of the pear family bearing fragrant yellow pear-shaped fruits which make delicious jewel-coloured jelly. Hard-boiled egg yolks rather than breadcrumbs were used for stuffing.

1.4 kg (3 lb) wild goose
150 ml (¼ pt) apple juice
2 tbsp quince jelly
150 ml (¼ pt) red wine
Salt and pepper

For the stuffing
1 Cox apple, peeled and chopped
1 Conference pear, peeled and chopped
4 hard-boiled egg yolks, diced or finely chopped
2 tbsp quince jelly
2 tbsp chopped parsley
1 tbsp chopped sage
½ tsp ground cinnamon
¼ tsp ground cloves

Pre-heat the oven to 180°C / 350°F / gas mark 4

Mix the ingredients for the stuffing and place in the body cavity of the goose.

Tie string round the parson's nose and then round the legs closing the entrance to the body cavity. Place the goose breast down on a rack in a roasting tin and pour over the apple juice. Cook for one hour. Turn the goose over, baste and cook for another hour. Brush the legs and breast with quince jelly and roast for a further 15 minutes. Using a spoon remove the stuffing from the goose then transfer it to a carving dish and keep warm.

Break up the stuffing with a fork and mix with the pan juices, and quince jelly. Add the red wine and seasoning and heat through to make the sauce.

Stuffed Goose Breasts

Serves 4

Stuffing each breast with flavoured sausage meat and wrapping with bacon rashers will make a meal for four people. Adding different ingredients to the stuffing may vary the flavour. Try sage and onion, sun-dried tomatoes and basil or chopped apple and mixed herbs.

Breast meat from one young goose
110 g (4 oz) pork sausages, skinned
1 tbsp chopped apricots
1 tbsp chopped walnuts
2 tsp chopped fresh sage
Melted butter or olive oil
8 rashers streaky bacon
2 tbsp red wine or stock
1 tbsp sage and apple jelly
Salt and black pepper

Pre-heat the oven to 180°C / 350°F / gas mark 4

Mix the chopped apricots, walnuts and sage with the sausage meat and divide in half. Make a pocket in each breast by cutting it lengthways taking care not to cut right through. Stuff half the sausage meat in each pocket. Brush with melted butter or oil and season with black pepper. Wrap 4 rashers of streaky bacon round each breast and place them on a large square of tin foil. Draw the foil up round the meat, add two tablespoons of red wine or stock then fold the foil to make a sealed parcel. Place in a roasting tin and bake for 1½ hours. Undo the parcel, transfer the breasts onto a carving board and cover to keep warm.

Tip the juice from the parcel into the roasting tin, add the sage and apple jelly, salt and pepper to make the gravy.

Carve slices across the breasts to reveal the sausage meat stuffing and serve with vegetables, gravy and apple sauce. This may also be eaten cold with apple or mango chutney and salads.

CHAPTER FIVE

Pigeon

Amazing Maize

Shooting pigeons on flailed maize is a form of decoying unknown in the days of the father of the sport, the late Major Archie Coats. Game cover is flailed in February, iron-hard kernels fly out like yellow grapeshot and speckle the ground: in a hungry month it feeds wild game birds while pigeons go mad for it. To waste it is a missed shooting opportunity, and free bird food for a month. Shame on those who plough it in on the second of February and then preach about how much the shooting man does for wild birds. Commercially astute estates let the pigeon decoying on the maize for enough rent to pay for drilling next year's crop. Make sure your house-proud farmer leaves it well alone until the last possible minute.

So there we were hot from a triumph the week before when sixty-one pigeons were bagged in a morning – you have to be quick with maize. The grains are large; in a hundred pecks the pigeon has a crop full and sits snoozing on the ploughing to digest. Sixty-one were more than enough for a sportsman and were enough to give the 'Greenhill', breast-only treatment and put in bags of six in the freezer. Then came news that three guns had shot 625 and that four other chaps on three fields had bagged an enormous 851. The question must be asked – Why? But, yes indeedy, maize is the stuff and has taken over from Archie Coats' spring drilling and clover leys as the bag filler.

By pure luck the hide was a cracker; back wind in some old leylandii in a little pocket in the dark shadows, no brambles in the way, and sitting on a three-legged stool with a wisp of dark net on four poles in front, the human figure was invisible even standing up. The static decoys are a collection of all the free samples amassed during forty years of journalism – some old relics in that lot, many of them museum pieces. The Pigeon Magnet needed an airing so it was fired up and rotating nicely in a clockwise direction. Trouble was that the cradles were 'arse about face' so the decoys would be flying backwards. I stood and puzzled mightily about this, scratching my head like the old fenman who thought 'aperitif' was a set of dentures and Sugar Diabetes a Welsh flyweight boxer. Of course one ought to have switched the terminals on the battery but in the meantime two dead birds were tied on with elastic bands – a bit raggedy-looking, but at least facing the right way.

The 'picture' looked pretty good, boosted by three new shells covered in flock material like wallpaper in an Indian restaurant. Under no circumstances will they shine – the curse of plastic decoys – and when there was a shower and the sun came out and my other artificials gleamed like gig lamps, these remained natural. Due to more technical wizardry one of them even moved its wings, a flick of movement that never fails to draw. The question is often asked if there comes a point when technology takes too much of the skill out of a field sport. Discuss...

The first three arrivals fell and then it began to go pear-shaped. They came battling in from the front in the teeth of a wind cold enough to cut through two Patagonias and a big coat as though they were a string vest. Wings half closed the birds hung motionless, swinging slightly from side to side: hard to work them out. Get the incomer above the muzzles, for surely it was dropping, but that did not work so well. Next try to hang on until they swung left or right to make them crossers but by then they were too close. The odd one tumbled but the empty cases piled up. Only a desperate man will blame his cartridges for duff shooting, but this was a batch of 24 gm of 8s won in a raffle, a bit light and dust shot but good enough had they been held straighter. In the end they stopped coming and for no end of shots fifty-seven were bagged. That was more than enough to carry and the freezer was also getting full.

It was time for a scientific experiment. Dusting off the bathroom scales I weighed all my pigeon gear. Gun, big coat, two hundred and fifty cartridges, magnet and battery, sack of netting, ditto poles, ditto decoys, slasher, seat, bag of bits and a weighty pork pie from the village shop came to eight stones (112 pounds). Even a man of steel cannot carry that lot far in one go so it is best for the modern decoyer to drive to within five paces of the hide.

Cold Pigeon

Like a blast from the ice cap the gale swept over the flat fen from the North, a cold quarter. 'The North wind doth blow and we shall have snow...' The pigeons would be battling into the fir wood; the perfect place to be and just for once the build-up went smoothly, no snags or cockups. It was an easy drive down the field to the hiding place where the gear could be dumped so no tedious carrying. The truck was left conspicuously at the other end to turn the birds this way; just about the only advantage in having a white vehicle, even one pebble-dashed with fen mud. Overhanging ivy gave a perfect backdrop and adjustable poles stood firm swathed in a petticoat of dyed hessian beneath a skirt of 'cammo' netting.

The first two birds veered away from a pale, human face so it was the work of a moment to get out the old shut knife and hack three small portholes in the netting. Now one could sit at ease and catch the first flicker of an incoming wing without being seen. So far so good but it was a shaky start. Shaky? Downright diabolical more like it. It took six shots to get one. Throw in a bit more swing. The gale made the birds toil but stand up to shoot one as you might on a calm day and it turned a wing and the wind tossed it fifty yards across the sky. Better hang on until the last minute when they were close, rise smoothly, take the chances and improve more than somewhat. It was warm in the lee of the dense trees and after removal of one of the three fleeces the intrepid shooter was a tad more mobile and less like a Michelin Man.

A few dead birds were set up out on the headland of the daffodil field where massed bands of golden trumpets faced the sun. A flicker of grey in front, get ready for another but it was a hen harrier and what a beauty. It is not often you see an adult male in full plumage: dove grey, snowy white and black wing tips, a handsome chap to be sure and what an honour but, almost taking my hat off, ten minutes later there was a sparrow hawk. Less welcome perhaps but he lives here, whereas the harrier will migrate and spread his favours.

The pigeons came in ones and twos, nothing heavy but you could never relax. Two special if fluky shots made my head spin in disbelief. Did I really get those? Shame that nobody was there to witness them; both dead in the air, high and curling, flung back by the gale to tumble way back on the daffs. Witnesses are all very well but they see your rubbish shots as well as your much rarer brilliant ones; you need to be able to turn spectators on and off as required. I sent China for each pigeon, a good exercise at long, unmarked retrieves.

At dusk there were seventeen for thirty-three cartridges, which, considering a dreadful start, was good enough.. Not one thorn tangled the netting, there was no mud, and the only weeny problem was the shooting stick that fell over each time I stood up to shoot. Not a bad way to spend an otherwise slow spring afternoon.

Home to Roost

The final shots of the last drive of the last day of the game shooting season had rolled round the covertside, faded into the distance and died. The silence was deafening, as it must have been on 11 November 1918 when the guns on the Western Front fell silent after five years of hellish thunder. However, the keen shooting man, woman or child with energy and enthusiasm undiminished after a January of cock shoots, keepers' days and fun knockabouts would be unwise to put his gun away just yet, for what connoisseurs consider the cream of shooting is about to begin.

If a pigeon coming into decoys presenting every shot in the book is a target for the expert, then its cousin lilting into the storm-tossed ash poles on a February night is a bird for the best. Cynics call roost shooting 'cartridge makers' benefits' for the ratio of kills per shot is nothing to boast about but when you do happen to send one tumbling down, the buzz you experience makes it worthwhile. Like decoying it is a one-man sport and the tactics are simple enough. Observation and experience will have shown you the best roosting woods, and pigeons have their favourites. Fir woods are popular as are half-dead trees swathed in ivy, for pigeons love the berries. Tall beech is popular as are willow woods. Halfway through a short winter's afternoon the birds leave their feeding grounds and might fly many miles following favoured landmarks until they arrive at the wood.

As in most field sports the weather is critical. On a stormy night the pigeons wish to escape the buffeting as soon as they can and drop directly into the topmost twigs and seek shelter. If the weather is balmy their natural caution kicks in and they circle endlessly scanning for danger. They are not foolish enough to do this within easy range but skim over like showers of arrows sixty yards up tempting the less experienced to have a pop. This rash shot has two results: the pigeon is handsomely missed, is taught a useful lesson and reminded that its initial caution was justified. Usually he will go elsewhere for a safer reception and take his mates with him. Next time he approaches a wood on a calm night he will be more circumspect. For roost shooting the rougher the night the better, so choose one when the gale screams through the trees and mighty boughs are ripped off and lie like severed limbs on the forest floor, and wait until the bird is in easy range. Exercise caution so as not to be flattened under a falling branch. On evenings of dead calm your time is better spent in the armchair by the fire watching the rugby.

Given a likely evening, the shooter ought to be in position by mid-afternoon. Do not be caught in the act of hide building or wandering about when the early birds arrive. The hide may be rudimentary. More harm than good is done by large, overcomplicated hides and a bulky hide where there was no hide the day before can be conspicuous. The best plan is standing still as pigeons are very good at spotting movement but remain mobile so you can change places quickly. Choose a place towards the downwind end of the wood as all birds land head to wind. It need not be clear overhead although many shooters perform fretfully when firing through a frieze of twigs. A gap in the canopy has advantages for the shot and is less likely to be spoiled by crossing branches but the moment a pigeon tops the clearing your upturned white face is visible and it will jink or flare and become unhittable. Anyone who has been hot-air ballooning or climbed a tall tree will testify how obvious the human face is when viewed from above. For a woody seeking a secure berth for the night, this apparition is a turnoff and will have it veering away in alarm. The message is to conceal the face behind a scrap of netting or clumps of strategically placed ivy and not twitch a muscle until the time comes to raise the gun smoothly and shoot. By this time the bird is committed and left it too late for violent evasion.

So there we are, well concealed by a fallen tree swamped with friendly, dark green ivy, face outline broken by leaves, gazing downwind whence the pigeons are likely to arrive. If you have a dog it should be sitting stone still beneath your cover but like most dogs in hides it will somehow have found a chink through which to watch proceedings. Dogs like to know what is going on. Distant shots show where other roost shooters are finding sport. This is no bad thing as it stops the flocks settling in any one place and attracting others, keeping them on the move. Early birds are in the air, darting across the heavens like grey arrows. Do not worry; as evening advances they will come in lower. Resist the urge to have hopeful shots at impossible targets for the only beneficiaries are the cartridge makers, along with more restrained shooters in woods nearby.

Here comes a possible one, lower and slower than the rest looking for a landing place. It passes overhead within shot and this time you rise smoothly and in a single movement swing through and fire. Do not worry about invasive twigs and branches; treat the shot as though it were in the open. If you make allowances for the overhead gap, you poke and miss every time. Let us say your luck and skill are both in; the bird emits a squirt of white feathers and comes clattering through the branches to lie demure in death amid the bluebells. Pigeons flying in to roost are tough targets and you have made a good shot. Like decoyed birds no two are the same so you get them crossing from both directions, coming in from straight ahead with the odd one setting its wings at enormous height and stooping in like a peregrine, pulling up just short of the treetops. If you can kill a bird for every three cartridges you are entitled to boast a little.

If at the end of a short winter's afternoon you have picked up a dozen you may pat yourself on the back. What is more, such birds are often fatter and in better condition than decoyed birds so are ideal for the kitchen. The late Mr Ken Gandy, the game dealer from Ely, reckoned that he could always tell whether a sack of pigeons had been decoyed or shot at roost. The decoyed birds might have been that bit hungrier, less cautious, not quite as aware of danger as the others.

Pigeon roost shooting in early spring is an exciting and challenging sport with a shotgun. Those who cannot be bothered with it and put up the shutters when the sun sinks on the first of February miss a great deal.

The Greenhill Method

This book is not a manual on game preparation but we do need to explain the Greenhill Method of preparing a pigeon for the pot. When you become handy you can render a pigeon oven-ready in fifteen seconds and use no knife, scissors or any tool. It was invented by that fine countryman Mr Ron Greenhill who resides in the 'Kingdom' of Reach in the sunny county of Cambridgeshire. It works best with a cold pigeon rather than a freshly shot one. A large apron and a pair of surgical gloves are recommended. This procedure assumes you are right-handed.

Working over a dustbin with a plastic bin liner inside, lie the bird breast down on your left hand. Seize the right wing and screw it off, pulling and tearing and drop it into the bin.

Turn the bird on its back and repeat the process with the left wing.

Holding the bird in your left hand, breast uppermost, seize the crop and pull it downwards tearing it off in one single, strong movement. Sometimes the head will come off; it matters not.

This operation will reveal a vee-shaped gap at the base of the neck where the wishbone is situated. Into this insert both thumbs and break the bird in half along its length. The back portions along with innards and the breast skin plus feathers will peel away easily after the initial break which takes a little strength.

Drop all the waste into the bin and you are left with the whole breast meat on the bone with loose feathers stuck to it. Pick these off and place the meat on a tray prior to moving smoothly on to bird number two. The meat may be frozen in packs and may be cut from the bone before cooking if the recipe requires it.

This is a delightfully simple system of bird preparation and far less complicated than it reads. After practising on about a dozen birds you will have acquired the knack and be delighted at how your speed improves.

Rifle, Rifle, Folderiddle-I-do...

In these times of plenty it is hard to imagine a shooting world in which cartridges, decoys, nets and other gear were not as cheap and available as now. In what some are pleased to call 'the good old days' pigeon decoys were solid, carved wooden ones or the primitive Max Baker type shells, if you could get them. There was no such thing as cammo netting and no telescopic hide poles. Cartridges cost twelve shillings (60p) a box of twenty-five when a farm worker's wage was a fiver a week. On the plus side there were a few places that could take your dead birds for a fair price. Those in the know kept the addresses quiet and dispatched their birds in hessian sacks on the train and waited for the cash to arrive – which it did within the week. If you shot straight you could make a little money although the margin was tight. The lucky ones tapped into a Ministry of Agriculture scheme whereby you got cheap cartridges for pest control. Many a one was fired at 'pests' with long tails but that is by the by. The government was keen to encourage sportsmen to shoot rabbits and pigeons when post-war farming was recovering.

The answer was the .22 rifle. This is what the Lincolnshire boys used for market gunning for it had all the advantages of being silent and deadly, the ammunition was cheap and with the short cartridge birds were not damaged. I had a Winchester pump action, fifteen shot 1895 model with tubular magazine and open sights of the sort used at fairground booths in the happy days before Health and Safety.

The field was a six-acre corner plot of badly drilled barley, what they used to call 'cuckoo corn', drilled late enough for the arriving cuckoo to have seen it go in. It would not have amounted to much. In those days farmers used the standard seed drill unlike the precision machines of today where no grain is wasted. Then, the corn was scattered

about as the seedbed was often ill-prepared and nubbly – a pigeon dining room with an open invitation to visit. Grains lay easily visible, ideal for pigeons which, unlike rooks, will never dig for a seed. Those soft beaks take only things they can see.

Boughs of willow and elder were perfect for a good hide in the hedge. A hide maker never cuts into hardwood trees or damages the stock-proof structure of a hedge, at least not if he wants to be invited again. A rifle could be poked through a chink and fired from the sitting position. It took a few minutes to throw down a few home-made decoys cut from sections of plastic guttering. Not very realistic and prone to shine they were good enough for unsophisticated pigeons in those days. A solid wooden carved one cost a tenner. A piece de resistance was the Magnificent Seven stuffed pigeon decoys, prepared from a method written up in the *Shooting Times*. They were kept in banks of cardboard shoeboxes for although extremely realistic, they were fragile. Those were times of make do and mend; modern shooters are spoiled for choice and have less need for inventiveness and ingenuity. Our mottos were 'Use it up, make it last, wear it out...'

Settling down on a backless kitchen chair, I slipped fifteen short rifle bullets into the magazine, poked the barrel through a narrow slit and settled down to wait. The cuckoo shouted his name from a hawthorn, a party of long-tailed tits chimed their bells and darted from frond to frond, hanging upside down seeking insects, calling incessantly, keeping the group together. Two mallard flew round and landed on the corn drill. They looked around, waddled a few paces in that peculiar rolling gait of wildfowl, and began to peck at the spilled grain.

The first pigeon was there as if by magic. A whirr and clatter of wings and he was down, staring suspiciously at the motionless decoys. Ease the barrel of the little rifle a touch to the left, squint down the sight, a gentle squeeze, a spit of a shot and the deadly crumb of lead speeds and the bird flaps and lies still. Click-clank, slide the pump action ready for the next, already there and waiting. Pigeons tend to flight to feed in long strings, one launches itself off the tree and beats a steady course; on the way it picks up others. Hearing the discharge of a 12-bore they will flare and depart but the spit of the rifle does not scare them and break up the flight line.

It turned out to be one of those days when all went to plan. The pigeons kept coming. Sometimes two landed at once, both fell, the first one slumping dead but not scaring the second. Now and then there was a walker, a wounded bird that plodded amongst the decoys making the 'picture' even more realistic. It was easy to fire at a bird on the ground with the second hovering over its head waiting to land but not scared off. There was a growing pile of spent brass cartridge cases in the leaf mould in the hide.

The trouble with the rifle method is the feathers. With a shotgun the birds are shot here and there, not often in the same spot, and the wind disperses the blown feathers. This field looked as if a snowstorm had hit it and half-way through the afternoon the pigeons began to veer away and the flight dried up. That was it. I counted exactly 216 good fat pigeons off that field and not a single one lost; a record that took many years to break. The birds were laid out to cool overnight and next day sacked and taken to the train at Ely station where they went north to their mysterious destination. Just for once a little cartridge money came back.

Cornfield Capers

The summer grew stale, corn turned from green to old gold and then russet, and that is when the pigeons found it. You can tell when the birds have found the corn for they sit on the high-tension cables that march across the great fields. From a distance the rows of dots look like a stave of music, undulating crotchets written by Chopin in extravagant mood. Watch this nocturne for a few moments and you will see pigeons launch themselves to where a flattened patch has given access to the grain.

The summer had been wet and windy, weather to make the stalks grow long and then fall down at the first wind, lying as flat as a pavement. The farmer could still harvest it as the modern combine is an amazing machine but the pigeons would get to it first. The cornfield pigeon is usually feeding young at the nest and there are those who prefer not to shoot birds, pests or not, that are feeding young, for at one shot you orphan a family and leave chicks to starve. Many shooters leave pigeons alone until autumn.

This farmer had pleaded for assistance so I sallied forth to help him, a knight in shining armour with a shotgun. Hide-making in summer is a doddle for the high bank-side vegetation is lush and elder bushes are in full leaf with dinner plate flowers to disguise the flash of human skin. Another virtue of elder is that flies cannot abide it so keep away. Buzzing flies can drive a shooter to distraction and insect repellent is a useful extra in the kit bag.

Decoys do not show well on flat corn, so the static picture needs a boost. What the incomers want to see is movement. This may be introduced in a variety of ways. From the dead bird on a long, springy wand that floats and dives in the breeze, known as a swooper or a flapper; wing movers, working on a long cord leading to the hide, had their day but the modern answer is the rotating pair of decoys known as the Pigeon Magnet. Anything which shows passing pigeons a flash of white brings them hurrying to the feast. Purists say that the mechanical flapper driven by a battery takes the field craft out of the job and debases decoying to a sport anybody can do. It is almost a good point but today I was there to kill a few pigeons so no scruples. My Magnet was rotating steadily, two decoys chasing each other in permanent and fruitless pursuit. The static decoys were dead ones saved and frozen in natural postures, the dead bird being by far the best decoy.

Pigeon were sitting in the ash tree on the corner of the field, others were buzzing across the heavens in a good flight line from the south-west. It would not be a long wait with so much traffic. A run of early customers drawn by the decoys came swinging in from the right, banked into the wind and set to land. Easy enough shooting and several paid the price. It is important when shooting in standing corn for your dead birds to fall on the flattened bit. The last thing the farmer needs is a leaden-footed decoyer tramping about in the standing crop searching for lost birds and doing more damage than the pigeons. A dog is not the answer for game is hatching and a dog in hot weather is uncomfortable and moves too much. By waiting until the first few clients were hovering over the middle of the decoys looking for a place to land I managed to drop nine of them on the flat corn. Waiting for a lull I went out to set them up, packing the small area with a mass of grey and white. Pigeon decoys in a small hole in laid corn may be set close together. You would not get away with it on an open field but when the available feeding space is small, pack 'em in...

As often happens the early rush was followed by a lull until a single bird almost caught me napping and fell, then another and one after another, no big rushes or flocks they dribbled in perfectly. There was the ripe perfume of bruised grass, the afternoon grew drowsy, the flight dried up and the world stood still. Well fed pigeons sat far off in the beeches in the squire's park; they would not return until just before bedtime. Time to pack up. One of the skills of decoying is knowing when to cut your losses and when to stick it out so I gathered thirty-one fine birds, collected my gear and tramped back to the green lane where the little van awaited me.

The dead pigeons were attracting the blowflies and the next job was to prepare them for the freezer before the eggs could hatch and spoil them. Archie Coats' advice was to go through them and pick off eggs from the beaks or open wounds. It is time-consuming and you just have to miss one lot and the bag is infested, but in the time it takes to use the Greenhill Method, you might as well do them properly and forget the flies.

Recipes

A vailable throughout the year there are many ways to cook pigeon. Cassell's *Dictionary of Cookery*, popular at the beginning of the twentieth century lists more than forty recipes. Most recipes only use the breasts so there is no need to pluck the bird. The quickest way is to use the Greenhill Method, described above which, in less than a minute, gives you all the breast meat on the bone, oven ready. No knife or scissors are required, only a strong pair of thumbs.

Choose only young pigeon or squabs for roasting; you can tell them by the lack of white collar. Place a quarter of an orange or some herbs inside each bird, smear a little butter on the breasts or wrap a rasher of bacon round each bird and roast at 200°C/400°F/gas mark 6 for 20 minutes. Remove the bacon, baste and cook for a further 10 minutes.

Either cook the meat on the bone, which helps to enrich the gravy or remove the whole breast and use the bones for stock to make soup or sauces. The breast meat may be cooked slowly for at least 1½ hours in a casserole or pie with any variety of vegetables but it is also excellent marinated for a few hours in olive oil, balsamic vinegar and herbs. To spice up the marinade add a teaspoon of chopped red chillies or root ginger then flash fry the breasts for about 3 minutes on each side so that they are still pink in the middle and succulent. Use the marinade, stock made from the breastbones, crème fraîche and a spoonful of honey to make a delicious sauce. Alternatively cut into thin slices for stir-frying. Allow a bird each if serving whole otherwise 6 whole breasts will serve 4 people.

Warm Pigeon Salad

Serves 4

The secret of a good salad, warm or cold, is to introduce a variety of textures to give it the 'crunch' factor with seeds, nuts or barely cooked vegetables. There is a good selection of salad leaves in the shops if you do not grow your own, including many varieties of lettuce, watercress, baby spinach or endive. Sesame seeds are harvested from an annual herb grown in Asia. Toasted seeds, high in protein, are crushed to make a wonderful, nutty oil used to flavour stir-fries and salads. This recipe includes a handful of pigeons, easily available at all times of year.

Breast meat from 6 pigeons sliced into strips
2 tbsp sunflower oil
1 yellow pepper, deseeded and sliced
1 red pepper, deseeded and sliced
1 small leek, finely sliced
1 large carrot, cut into fine strips
3 tsp sesame seeds
6 handfuls baby spinach or lamb's lettuce
2 tbsp toasted sesame oil
1 tbsp white wine vinegar
1 tbsp soy sauce
Salt and ground black pepper

Heat the oil in a frying pan or wok. Add the pigeon and stir-fry for 3 minutes. Add the chopped vegetables and sesame seeds and stir-fry for 3 minutes. In a bowl whisk together the sesame oil, wine vinegar, soy sauce, salt and pepper. Add the spinach or lamb's lettuce, warm pigeon and vegetables and toss together so that the ingredients are well coated with the dressing. Serve at once with new potatoes or crusty bread.

Pigeon Hotpot

Serves 4

Hotpot is a Lancashire dish traditionally cooked in an earthenware pot packed with meat and vegetables topped with a layer of potatoes. The breast meat is cooked on the bones and these are removed halfway through the cooking time.

4 whole pigeon breasts
2 rashers bacon, chopped
1 large onion, finely chopped
2 large carrots, peeled and cut into rings
225 g (8 oz) mushrooms, sliced
2 cloves garlic, crushed
600 ml (1 pt) pigeon or chicken stock
1 tbsp fresh thyme
Salt and black pepper
Oil for frying
900 g (2 lbs) potatoes peeled and sliced

Pre-heat the oven to 180°C/350°F/gas mark 4

Heat the oil in a frying pan. Soften the onions and then cook the chopped bacon.

Transfer to a casserole and add the pigeon breasts, carrots, mushrooms, garlic, stock, thyme and seasoning. Cover and cook for 1 hour. When cool enough to handle remove the pigeon breasts and cut the meat from the bone. Slice each breast into 4 and return the meat to the casserole. Check the seasoning. Cook the potatoes for 10 minutes then cut into slices. Place them in layers on top of the casserole and season well. Cover and bake for a further hour, removing the lid for the final 15 minutes to brown the potatoes. Serve with a green vegetable.

Red Thai Pigeon

Serves 4

All the ingredients for this dish may be bought from the supermarket. To save time you may prefer to buy a jar of Thai curry paste which, once opened, will keep in the fridge for a month.

Breast meat from 6 pigeons
1 tbsp olive oil
2 x 200 ml (14 fl oz) coconut cream
2 tbsp Thai fish sauce
1 tsp sugar
1 tbsp chopped coriander

For the curry paste
1 stalk lemon grass
2 red chillies, deseeded
Zest and juice of a lime
3 shallots, peeled
2 cloves garlic
2.5 cm (1 inch) piece of root ginger, sliced
½ tsp ground cumin
½ tsp ground coriander

Finely slice the lemon grass and leave to soak in the lime juice for 1 hour.

Place this and all other ingredients for the curry paste in a food processor and grind to a paste.

Heat the oil in a frying pan. Cook the pigeon breasts for 2 minutes on each side. Remove from the pan and cut each breast into 4 or 5 slices. Add the curry paste to the pan then slowly add the coconut cream stirring all the time on a high heat so the sauce reduces slightly. Stir in the fish sauce, sugar and pigeon slices. Simmer for 5 minutes to allow the pigeon to heat through. Finally stir in the chopped coriander.

Serve with fragrant Thai rice.

Sweet and Sour Pigeon

Serves 4

This is a good recipe for using less than perfect birds as the breast is cut into strips so any damaged meat may be discarded. It also works well with pheasant and is a tasty way to introduce children to the delights of game.

Breast meat from 6 pigeons
2 tbsp olive oil
1 large red pepper, deseeded and sliced
1 tbsp lime juice
2 tbsp soy sauce
2 tbsp orange juice
2 cloves garlic, crushed
1 tbsp clear honey
Black pepper

Cut each breast into 4 slices. Toss the sliced meat in 1 tablespoon of the olive oil and the lime juice. Season with black pepper.

Mix together the soy sauce, orange juice, garlic and honey. Heat the other tablespoon of oil in a frying pan and stir-fry the red pepper for 4 minutes. Add the pigeon meat and stir-fry for another 4 minutes. Pour the soy mix over the pigeon and cook for a further 4 minutes. The sauce will reduce and thicken slightly.

Delicious served with noodles or rice and a green salad.

Pigeon with Dark Chocolate

Serves 4

Chocolate is not as sinful as once supposed. Any with a cocoa content of 60% or more has a superior taste and is a good source of magnesium, iron and flavonoids, which are antioxidants and may help reduce the risk of a heart attack.

As well as making mouth-watering cakes and puddings, chocolate may be used in savoury dishes. Added at the last minute it gives a rich flavour and smooth velvety texture to a casserole or sauce. The Italians use it in hare stew served with pasta. Here the addition of a small amount of strong dark chocolate makes an unusual sauce to accompany pigeon breasts. The sauce may have the appearance of melted chocolate ice cream but the taste is quite different.

Breast meat from 6 pigeons
Oil for frying
6 tbsp red wine
3 tbsp balsamic vinegar
2 tsp English mustard
15 g (½ oz) dark chocolate (at least 60% cocoa)
4 tbsp crème fraîche
Garlic salt
Pepper
Chopped parsley for garnish

Heat the oil in a frying pan. Cook the pigeon breasts for 3 minutes on each side. Leave to rest in a warm oven.

Deglaze the pan with the red wine then add the balsamic vinegar, mustard, garlic salt and pepper. Bring to the boil, add the chocolate and stir until melted. Blend in the crème fraiche and heat through gently. Adjust the seasoning if necessary. The sauce should be smooth with a bittersweet flavour.

Spoon a little sauce over the meat and sprinkle with chopped parsley. Serve the rest of the sauce separately.

CHAPTER SIX

Various

Rookery Nook

My childhood was closely bound with rooks. The bedroom overlooked the shrubbery across the lawn in which marched a stately line of elms and lime trees, home to the vicarage rookery. Lying in my truckle bed on a spring morning was better than watching the TV we did not have. Each bird was a personality and I came to know them and their bulky nests of twigs. Some of them were well-behaved and good neighbours, weaving the unwieldy sticks into their structure with care. Turn their backs for a moment and a rascally neighbour would slip in and steal the material. If the burglar were caught red-handed a battle would follow – lots of bad language and flying feathers. Some of them were quarrelsome, some easygoing, some were home-breakers flirting with the spouses of others. After the spring fever of bonding they settled into the routine of incubation and food gathering. High above the granite gravestones in the swinging nest the hen would crouch, the five spotted eggs clutched between her thighs while her mate foraged on grass verges and in meadows for cockchafer grubs and wireworms.

One day in late March the querulous calls came from the first hatchlings and within a week the cries grew stronger and came from more nests. The food gathering became an endless shuttle as parent birds came and went – no time now for the wife-swapping and shenanigans of the turn of the year. The squabs grew bigger until they were old enough to take a few steps off the nest, grip the twigs with their scaly feet and gaze round at the new world. Now they became 'branchers' and their cries for food were heart-rending and their parents began to look a little frayed.

All this I saw as from the bed, a soap opera played out for my personal delectation with an episode every day. Then one sad evening in May the squire came round with his pals and the spit of the rifles and boom of the 12-bores saw my friends, the black ragged bundles, tumbling into the cow parsley and young nettles. No doubt I made a touching sight leaning on the windowsill clutching a tear-stained handkerchief. The farmers argued that they were controlling a pest but while the rook takes the odd partridge egg and will dig for grain, it is insect pests that make up its main diet. Once a freak swarm of locusts appeared without warning near Craven in Shropshire. Rooks flocked in thousands and mopped them up. An inexplicable plague of caterpillars appeared on Skiddaw – so many that they threatened to destroy every scrap of greenery on the hill but rooks discovered the feast and polished off the lot. As for eggs – pheasants, moorhens, coots, hawks, hedgehogs, redlegs, herons and bitterns – the list of opportunist egg eaters is endless, so are we to eliminate them all? Those who rear twenty thousand game birds a season are not going to argue that the handful of early eggs taken by the rook demands slaughter of the whole tribe. In fact the rook does you a favour, for the second brood of pheasant and partridge has a better chance when the vegetation has grown. Keepering should seek to make friends not enemies of the public.

Rooks love people and nest close to their habitations and places of worship. In their baggy trousers and shiny black undertakers' suits they waddle on the grass verges stuffing insects into their beak pouches, unfazed by traffic thundering within feet and rarely are run over. They are sagacious birds. It is said, and there are case histories, that they can foretell the death of the householder and will fly to a great height cawing wildly and desert the place for some years. They are able to predict the weather, rooks spiralling up on a great thermal tell of settled weather but when they caw wildly and fly aimlessly hither and thither then look out for storms. They have parliaments and courts of justice, and let you know when a tree is dying though you cannot see it for yourself. They detect a lessening of pliancy in the topmost twigs and do not nest in it. They fly like angels, argue garrulously but have countless friends, love their spouses, are devoted to their scrofulous children and the whole year long brighten our days with their cheerful cawing, crowing, squawking and crooning. Leave him alone and welcome him; regard it as an honour to have him nest on your property for you are one of the chosen ones. The rook is family and some of his habits mirror our own.

The rook's housing market fell on hard times for his traditional elms caught a hideous disease and perished. Ever a survivor his tenements appear in clumps of scrub ash in the middle of motorway roundabouts. The elms in the old vicarage garden are long

gone, along with the house itself. Where for a century generations of rooks swung in the branches, flew above the gravestones of the forefathers of the village and watched the comings and goings of their descendants, now their trees are hideous, truncated ruins.

This is a book with a cooking theme and it must not be forgotten that rook pie was and still is a traditional dish of spring. The young are certainly good to eat given the correct recipe and I see nothing wrong in the sportsman going out to bag enough to make a traditional pie for are we not hunter-gatherers? This does not mean a random slaughter of the innocents whose bodies are left to rot but a judicious harvesting of a shootable surplus.

Japanese Sniper

The common snipe is a magical bird, not to be confused with its cousin the jack snipe. Winston Churchill liked to make a breakfast of a couple (never a brace), of snipe on toast, trail intact of course, washed down by a bottle of Bolly. Not many can run to such patrician tastes these days although a snipe does make a tasty titbit if properly cooked. The jack snipe is a little smaller, shorter in the bill, protected and has too often been confused with its larger relative. The jack flies a short distance without zig-zagging and pitches close by so in the old days when the bird was a legal mark you might walk it up and have another go. There is a beautiful story of an Irish butcher who rented rough shooting on a vast bog. It was as good as devoid of game but one jack snipe lived there. Each time the butcher sallied forth with his muzzle-loader the bird would rise, fly straight and slowly and pitch again, as is its way.

The butcher was an execrable shot and missed it every time. It landed nearby so he was able to reload and walk it up again with the same result. In this way that one jack snipe gave him a whole season's shooting for it survived until closing day. The day after the season ended the butcher took a stroll across his shoot in the company of a friend carrying a walking stick instead of his gun. Sure enough the snipe rose again as it had for the previous eight weeks. 'Look, there's my old pal,' cried the butcher throwing his stick playfully in the bird's direction. You may have guessed ... by some outrageous fluke the stick caught the poor snipe amidships and brought it down.

Mass drainage by stern-faced authorities that cannot abide an old-fashioned plashy water meadow has all but done for the snipe population. You may shoot at a species all you like and it comes back stronger, but take away its habitat and it is doomed. There are a few hallowed places where it thrives and even some driven snipe shoots that have operated in much the same way for a hundred years. The Arundel Arms in Devon has some old snipe driving ground as does at least one estate on Anglesey. I have

seen two hundred snipe in the air at once on Orkney and almost as many in parts of West Wales and Devon. When the Ouse Washes in Cambridgeshire were knee-deep to a wader, the heavens were alive with them, their 'scaaape scaape' sounding like so many nanny goats. It is rare these days to find a dozen. Once I shot a common snipe with Michael Dawnay in Wales that had a ring on its leg showing that it had been trapped and ringed as a juvenile on the island of Heligoland, so it had come some fair distance. There has been a decline in old-fashioned rough shooting where a couple of sportsmen with a leash of spaniels would wander here and there shooting what they flushed. Most game-holding ground now is incorporated into the local driven shoot. The result is that a bag on a driven shoot might contain a couple of snipe and rarely more unless it is one of the specialist snipe shoots. In the nineteenth century when most bags comprised grey partridges and snipe, the great Irish snipe shots like the legendary O'Halloran would kill nine out of ten with his hammer gun.

The keen snipe shot might have to cast his eyes overseas to find his sport and thus it was that I found myself on the shores of the Caspian Sea near an Iranian seaside town of Chalus, where a patchwork of paddy fields ran down to the water. The political situation now is tenser but the Iranians we met were nothing but charming, courteous, honest and helpful, far from the 'Axis of Evil' that President Bush had told us to expect. With my bird boy Mohammed at my side we crouched by a low bank that marked a paddy field boundary. Two hundred yards away a mixed team of beaters and pointers lined out and quietly came forward.

That little patch erupted snipe, common and jacks and like so many paper darts they shot overhead squeaking alarm. Shots rang out and the odd bird arrowed to earth to be gathered by the eager lads. When I missed two in succession Mohammed gave me a good talking to and, in sign language, a lecture on forward allowance. As an experience at shooting driven snipe it was rare, and how it must have been in the Fens in the pre-drainage days.

Unlike most forms of game shooting hitting driven snipe is easier then shooting them walked up. The old trick was to walk snipe downwind for they rise into it and you have a chance to fire if you can wait until the bird has stopped jinking. Rough weather is best as they tend to sit tight. Once you have flushed a good wisp from a water meadow wait patiently by a clump of rush and soon they come lilting back to give you a second chance. Hard frost is another likely time if you can find a freshet of open water but they can stand only so much of it. After a week they move to the coast or westwards to find more open conditions. Another interesting fact is that for such a tiny bird a snipe can carry shot well and needs to be well hit. A pellet that would drop a grouse in its tracks might leave a snipe departing apparently unscathed.

The snipe remains a fair mark for the modern sportsman but it must not be overdone. Take your couple by all means, cook them carefully and traditionally and share the pleasures experienced by the great Sir Winston. Should you catch them with their guard down in a sudden concentration or when bitter weather has brought them to the only open ditch in the county, it is wise, sporting and prudent to stay your hand and go easy.

Golden Reign

The golden plover was and is a fair mark, delicious on the table. It may still be shot and there are those in the West Country who value goldie shooting above any other. I know one man who comes across from Michigan every year especially for that obscure sport.

Well hidden behind his frieze of rush and reed the fen gunner peered at the half flooded meadow before him. On it stood a squad of what he called 'stales', models of golden plover carved out of wood, facing the wind like a platoon of dragoons. His old fenman's hairy ears pricked for far off he heard the melancholy double whistle; the first lot was on its way. Horny thumb snapped back the hammers on his old Cogswell, a fugitive from a better gun cabinet, and he gripped his ebony plover whistle, a treasured family heirloom, with his teeth. There they were, a tight knit group of about fifty golden plovers, flying purposefully towards the field that all week they had been using. He blew his whistle, a seductive, lilting call said by the old plover netters to be deadly. Hard to tell whether he needed it or not for they came direct to the decoys, twenty feet up looking to land. The skill of the old gunners was not to waste a cartridge at a single bird but to aim a true fowler's shot at the leader when they were nicely strung out and tightly packed, and maybe knock down half a dozen.

Old Will was a master and rising smoothly he swung ahead of the leaders, conscious of a mass of purposeful black arrows behind them and fired. Mortally stricken, several tumbled to flutter on the sward while the rest – another habit for which the golden plover is known – dived towards the ground still holding the direction of flight. Will knew what was coming and took a second chance and this time three more clattered to join those already down. It was a good start and he rushed out to gather his runners returning to the hide to await the next lot. His two shots had produced eleven birds and these would fetch a good price in the London market where he would send them in a hessian sack on the train.

As he waited he thought of his old dad who used to catch them in nets set for peewits. This was a regular job on the old fen and a serious money-spinner. In his best week he made over seventy pounds from plovers when a farm labourer earned a pound. In dry times the old man would flood a patch of low-lying washland to attract them. He did this by releasing a slacker to allow the water to gurgle in. In wet times he would build a small eminence of turves just big enough to be covered by his clap net and on this incomers would settle. They prefer landing on dry ground and walking into the water. Like all his gear his nets were home-made, woven by him in the cart shed, his netting needle a blur as he worked. The poles of the net were of ash cut from the tree by the house and the steel springs to give it that extra flick were fragments of cart spring begged from the blacksmith. He used the same whistle that his son used today.

He too used 'stales' crudely whittled from wood but best of all were birds he caught and tamed. Many found it surprising that such a wild spirit as a wader, used to travelling the flyways of the globe, might be tamed so easily. He selected a handful of peewits, goldies and sometimes a ruff, not uncommon then, and kept them in the dark in the shed feeding them on bread and milk. Some old Fenners did this with all their catch and the birds fattened amazingly and they fetched a better price. Those who feel sniffy about the morals of it, reflect that those were hard and hungry times with mouths at home to be fed. Scruples were a luxury for the round-bellied.

Will's old dad kept a few tame birds to use as decoys. Nothing would better convince wild ones that all was well, than the sight of their mates sitting contentedly on the flooded grass. One cunning trick involved attaching the live decoy to a wicker pan fixed to the end of a miniature seesaw. This was done by passing a thin reed through its crooked knees, fixing it in the sitting position. A long line linked the device to the netter hidden in his hide. Movement is a great attractor as any decoyer knows and when he saw far off a flock of plover lilting over the bank and aiming to pass him by, he pulled the cord. The decoy lifted from the ground and, unable to stand and pulled off balance, would flap its wings and wail. The flash of white and the call caught the eyes of the wild ones and brought them in. Some of his decoys became so tame that he had no need to keep them enclosed. They would follow him round the garden when he was digging, scuttling about under the very tines of the fork, gobbling earthworms and leather jackets.

Will's old dad owned a long barrelled 8-bore made by that amazing maker Mr Tolley. He loved to tell the story of one of his best shots at golden plover made on the muds of an Essex estuary. The gun was laid flat on a small open punt known locally as a 'shout' and the triggers were wired together to give a simultaneous discharge. He was on the lookout for a spring of teal huddled in a corner or a paddling of mallard in the lee of a mud bank but, rounding the spit in the thin mist, he came upon a stand of goldies, all at attention facing the wind. He lay down, steadied the boat and lining up the thickest saw that they were on the point of rising; one or two were stretching their wings. In two seconds it would be too late. His double gout of tawny flame and billow of iron grey smoke belched over the marsh with a twin boom that set the gulls complaining and the echoes rolling. His double shot cut a swathe through the thick of them and it took him a while but in the end he gathered thirty-seven; that meant he could buy shoes for his children. There were tales of fully blown punt guns knocking down a hundred or more to one shot so tightly do they cluster at the roost. Today the market gunners have gone and not many punters bother with goldies.

Nowadays the birds over-winter in the United Kingdom and it is possible to see flocks of thousands on the winter drills often on the same ones they visited last year. They have their favourite staging posts before travelling on, going north in spring and south in winter. Not many shoot them these days and many modern shooters would not recognise a golden plover if it fell onto their heads. Apart from snipe and woodcock it is the only wader we may still shoot, a perverse decision by those set in authority over us who took from the coastal gunner the curlew, redshank and grey plover (the peewit has been protected for much longer), but left the goldie on the list.

Today the small number shot has no effect on the overall population although its wandering habits make it a hard bird to track and count. It remains a far mark for the longshore gunner walking in his grandfather's footsteps and, as with the common snipe, there is no harm in shooting a handful for the pot. They remain as good to eat now as when the eminent Victorians pursued them in flat, grey punts with their great guns across the muds flats of the northern firths.

'Thim Owd Cutes...'

Two minor players in the shooting chef's repertoire are those common water-fowl – the coot and moorhen. It was not always so for the coot on a windy day was a target for royalty – literally – for King George VI and his father were keen coot shooters. I have in my collection a Purdey cartridge stamped with a red crown liberated from the royal ammunition bag by Jim Vincent who loaded for him at a Norfolk coot shoot. The coot shoots on Hickling Broad in Norfolk were famous, invitations keenly sought and people queued up on the shore to spectate, help and, with luck, retrieve and hide a bird missed by the dogs. The organisation was a major headache involving the begging, borrowing or impounding of any boat no matter how leaky. Then you prayed for calm weather for a storm meant cancellation. The shooters were spread amongst the boats, each with a stout oarsman or man with a quanting pole. Forming a wavy line on the downwind side of the great broad they set off, moving slowly upwind towards the far shore.

Ahead of this armada swam a flotilla of coots, not yet alarmed but simply putting distance between themselves and the old enemy. Keeping as good a line as possible with such a mixed armada the coots were pushed on, reluctant to break back between their pursuers. Eventually they were too close to the far shore for comfort, they dared not swim back between the boats so first one, then another then in ragged bands of half a dozen they rose, caught the wind and sailed back over the boats to the broad bosom of the lake behind. As the birds broke back they offered sporting shots. The guns volleyed, boats rocked wildly, boatmen did their best to hold their craft steady, black powder smoke hung heavily writhing like mist on the water as during the battle of Trafalgar.

The surviving coots flew back and landed far behind. The boats were trimmed, turned round, the line reformed and off they set again, chasing the birds to the far shore where the process was repeated. On the way the boatmen gathered dead ones that lay bobbing on the water, the odd bang showing where a 'diver' had been polished off. Again the boats drew close to the far shore and again the coots rose in ragged lines and streamed back, upwind this time so they climbed higher providing more sporting shots. Whole communities were involved in the coot shoots for in rural Norfolk excitement was hard to come by. Bank holidays, especially Boxing Day were favourites for this event. Sometimes a second line of local guns would be standing on the shore to join in the fun. At the Slapton Ley coot shoot in Devon in January 1891 1700 coots fell to twenty guns – said to be an English record.

• • •

HARDLY ANYONE SHOOTS A COOT TODAY although it is legal quarry and should one fly over on a duck shoot or be flushed off a pond it is likely to fall. If this happens it is incumbent on the one who shot it to take it home and eat it, otherwise he ought not to have fired. As a table bird in the eighteenth and nineteenth centuries its strong, marshy taste was popular and like most waterfowl, birds from freshwater tasted better than those feeding on salt marshes. Today it provides a shot for a hungry sportsman, adds variety to the bag and allows the gourmet to wander awhile in the steps of ancient sportsmen.

The common moorhen is familiar to many a shooter and was probably the first bird at which he raised a gun as a boy. It is not hard to shoot and makes a splendid mark for a beginner with a ·410, rising as it does in panic from the rushes, spluttering across the water, legs trailing. Contrary to common belief it does have a close season and may not be shot in the summer. Years ago in hard and hungry times many a marshman kept the pangs of hunger at bay by finding a moorhen nest, cracking the eggs onto a shovel and frying them on an open fire of dead willow twigs; such vital protein was not to be wasted.

Its name has nothing to do with moors but is a corruption of 'merehen', a bird found all round the world but not in vast deserts. Every waterway has a population and the cheery flirting of the two-fingered, white, tail salute is a mark of the summer and gives vibrancy to an otherwise lifeless water. The birds are good to eat and remain popular in certain kitchens, tasting very like beefsteak although you need a good few to make a 'pudden'. The problem is that like coots they possess an underlay of black dowl, minute feathers that no human fingers can pluck and little short of a blowlamp can remove. They must be skinned and this renders them unsuitable for anything except stews.

While not especially gregarious moorhens gather for good feeding in hard weather. They annoy keepers and feeders of duck ponds for they find the grain and mop it up before their nobler relatives arrive. We had a minor moorhen shoot when numbers had risen unacceptably high and they swarmed over the game food during bitter frost. Battling about in the rushes with busy spaniels and a couple of pals we flushed several and shot them down, not the most testing targets but a revisiting of sport as it used to be. We ended with seventeen, thinning them out but leaving a viable population. They are good for dogs to retrieve as they have a strong and attractive scent.

Those birds were skinned before the sun went down and mixed into a mighty 'oystercock' pie, good enough for fowlers and 'all honest men' as the great Izaak Walton said.

Springes to Catch Woodcock...

The Stetchworth Park shoot near Newmarket is special in many ways but notably for the fact that when a woodcock lifts nobody bellows, 'Woodcoooook!' and nobody ducks. The reason is that on that delectable estate woodcock are not shot at all, so the appearance of the dear old 'ditch owl' causes no more excitement than a blackbird. Possibly because of this the place is lifting with the things so you have to beat them off with a stick. On an end of season cocks-only day you might see fifty, seven or eight on each drive. Even a bungler might have got a dozen including a doddle of a right and left and there is no rule that says one may not swing the gun, aim and mutter 'bang-bang' under one's breath.

Not often having seen so many 'cock in one day in the same place, many of them present easy shots. Those that passed in the open flew in straight, level flight and not very fast, one or two darting up or down as they met the trees. Are woodcock as challenging and difficult to shoot as they say? In amongst trees maybe, but once they hit open country they can be easy. I have been lucky enough, and it is mostly luck, to shoot three rights and lefts with witnesses. The first was when I was a boy with a hammer gun, both barrels true cylinder, on a farmers' shoot in the next village. They were my first woodcock, the first ever on that shoot and the only ones seen that day so pure good fortune. In those days there was the 'Bols Snippen Club' and you got a bottle of liqueur, a tie, a badge and, for an extra fiver, a set of engraved liqueur glasses. The second pair I shot in Suffolk walking up pheasants when a couple rose from a dyke but I had only one witness. The third was in Devon with The Warrener, Pat Carey, and this time I had two witnesses but no amount of hunting with a pack of dogs could produce the second bird which appeared to fall as dead as last week so it did not count.

Others have been equally unlucky. One chap killed his second bird and looked round triumphantly to see a neighbour breaking his gun and ejecting a smoking case. Another shot two when sent on his own round the corner of the wood on a driven day; nobody saw him do it. People have elected to shoot the hardest bird first and gone on to miss the sitter with the second barrel. Sometimes a bird is not found or is carried away in a river and lost. Gareth Edwards, the rugby star, has done it three times on small bag days but the pair seems to pick him out every time as accurately as he found the All Black try line. It is a fluky business to shoot two with two witnesses and to pick up both birds. Members of the *Shooting Times* Woodcock Club are to be congratulated as much for luck as skill.

I have friends who do not raise the gun to a 'cock and I am wondering if the time has come to join them. I love to eat them and trail on toast is one of my favourites but I suppose I would live if denied it. One day I might give them a rest.

• • •

THERE IS AN OLD DEBATE ABOUT SHOOTING WOODCOCK on their evening flight out to feed. Some experts defend it while others find it harder to justify. I have never shot a woodcock on flight but not for want of trying. Waiting like a coiled spring in front of a black wood staring at the inky sky, finger on trigger, and from nowhere there comes a black dart that arrows past. Reactions are slow at the best of times so the bag remains empty. Ace woodcock man Michael Dawnay has no qualms and likens it to flighting wild duck onto a pond in the evening. Flighted 'cock are hard to hit so I guess that not many are shot but, if pressed, one might admit to a sneaky feeling that it is not quite cricket. If you have been chasing them all day, driving them from blocks of trees or walking them up over dogs they have given you good sport. To await nightfall and ambush them again when they are neither wary nor elusive but flying in a straight line out to feed is a blow below the belt – even if they are difficult to hit. A woodcock at any time is an occasion and a special bird. One should not tell others what they ought not to do, there are too many people doing that already, but I suspect that if invited to flight woodcock again I might well go early to the pub. I would not hit one anyway.

The woodcock is a brilliant bird, wonderful on the table as long as you cook it with trail intact in the old way. It was thought by ancients to be foolish as its moonstone eyes are set on top of its head and they glow when you shine a lamp across the meadows at night. It flies across the North Sea under the full November moon, it has been found in the stomachs of cod and caught in trawl nets. It lands on the Norfolk coast and continues to drift westwards and is plentiful although little research has been done to establish its precise population, a task as easy as catching smoke in a bottle. The pure magic of the bird is encapsulated by Richard Jefferies in *The Amateur Poacher* when he describes himself and his friend Orion shooting the woodcock on Farmer Willum's land under the nose of the hated neighbouring keeper. Delicious to eat, with plumage every shade of brown known to the Almighty, shootable on a rough day or a driven game shoot, the bird is a marvel and long may it remain to delight us and give us our sport.

Recipes

Woodcock, snipe and plover are difficult to shoot and are prized for their unique and distinctive flavours. All waders need to be plucked carefully as the skin is tender and tears easily. Make a small cut just below the breastbone and hook out the gizzard. Remove the crop and eyes and skewer the body and legs with the bill. Traditionally these small birds are not drawn before roasting but the trail is removed after cooking, mixed with brandy and perhaps a little pâté or cooked chicken livers and served on toast. In France this is known as 'a la mode classique'.

The French have a special regard for woodcock and use a silver funnel to pour a measure of calvados down its throat immediately after it is shot. The brain is considered to be the best part: the guns stand in a circle, the bird is placed on a stick and spun round. Whichever shooter the beak is pointing at gets to take this delicacy home. An unusual way of presenting 'becasse' given to me by a Frenchman is to put a clove of garlic inside the bird then cook it in butter in a pan for 20 minutes. When cool take the meat off the bone, discard the gizzard and keep the entrails. Place the meat including the trail, an equal amount of butter and 200 ml (6½ fluid ounces) of cream in a food processor and whizz. Put the mixture back in the pan, add salt and pepper and cook slowly until it starts to thicken. Take a baguette, slice and toast it, then spread the woodcock over the toast and pop under the grill until it starts bubbling. A couple of woodcock will serve two as a main course.

The trouble with snipe is the difficulty of obtaining enough at a time to feed more than one hearty eater. Winston Churchill's favourite breakfast was a couple of snipe washed down with champagne. The breast meat may be added to other meat for a game casserole or pie, although that is a waste of such a tasty morsel. Another dodge is to thread whole snipe and bacon rolls onto skewers, baste well and cook on the barbecue. Hugh Pollard writing on 'What Every Good Cook Should Know About Snipe' in *Country Fair* in 1951, recommended scooping out the two halves of a large and shapely potato to form a suitable coffin. The bird was placed in the 'coffin' with a knob of butter and baked in the oven or the embers of a fire. He also recommends snipe fried in bacon fat with cakes of fried mashed potato or parsnips cut into thin fingers or chips. A couple of snipe provide a modest breakfast or starter for two.

Plover have a delicate and fine flavour and have been eaten in this country for centuries usually in an enormous game pie along with various other game birds and wildfowl. More recently, a traditional supper for coastal wildfowlers was oystercock pie prepared by their landlady using the birds including wildfowl and assorted waders shot that morning on the shoreline. Like woodcock and snipe, plover are roasted without being drawn. Mrs Beeton recommended brushing them with butter, tying a thin slice of fat bacon over each breast and hanging them on the spit feet downwards with toast underneath to catch the drippings from the trail. They should be basted frequently and cooked for about 15 minutes then served on the toast garnished with watercress. Cook at 200°C/400°F/gas mark 6 in a modern oven!

Moorhen are impossible to pluck unless they are still warm when the feathers and down are more easily removed. Skinning is the easier option and as there is little flesh on the legs it is less bother just to remove the breast meat.

Moorhen are best when they have been feeding on stubbles. They may be included in a mixed game pie or casserole and I have read of shooters who, being uncertain of the flavour, have cooked it in a curry sauce.

Roast Woodcock

Serves 2

Snipe may also be used in this recipe but reduce the cooking time to 15 minutes.

A couple of woodcock
25 g (1 oz) softened butter
4 rashers streaky bacon
1 tbsp brandy
Salt and black pepper
2 slices bread, toasted
Lemon wedges for garnish

Pre-heat the oven to 200°C/400°F/gas mark 6

Cover the birds with the softened butter and season with black pepper. Wrap two rashers of bacon round each bird covering the breast and thighs. Place them in a small roasting tin and cook for 20 minutes. Remove the bacon rashers, baste and return to the oven for 5 more minutes. Transfer to a serving plate and allow the birds to rest for 5 minutes.

Remove the insides with a teaspoon, chop up the trail, add the brandy, salt and pepper and spread onto two slices toast. Place each woodcock on the toast, garnish with a slice of lemon and serve with thin gravy made from the pan juices.

Stuffed Woodcock

Serves 2

This is for the slightly squeamish who do not relish eating the trail. If you prefer to remove the head then use string to secure the legs to the parson's nose.

A couple of drawn woodcock
25 g (1 oz) butter
250 g (8 oz) pork sausage meat
1 dessert apple, peeled, cored and chopped
1 tbsp fresh thyme
1 tbsp fresh parsley
1 tbsp lemon juice
1 tbsp crab apple jelly
Salt and pepper

Pre-heat the oven to 180°C/350°F/gas mark 4

Mix the apples and herbs with the sausage meat and place half in each body cavity. Skewer the legs together with the bill and spread butter on each breast and legs. Dust with salt and pepper. Place the birds in a roasting tin and cook for 40 minutes. This is a longer time and lower heat than usual to ensure the sausage meat stuffing is cooked through. Transfer the birds to a serving dish, keep warm and rest for 5 minutes.

Stir the lemon juice, crab apple jelly, salt and pepper into the pan juices and heat through to make a thin gravy.

Rook Pie

Serves 4

There is no close season for rooks and traditional rook shoots were held in early May to thin out squabs or branchers before they left the rookeries later in the month. Rook pie was a once a year treat for country folk short of meat. Only the breast meat from young birds, which is pale, tender and mild flavoured, is considered to be worth eating. As the taste is fairly bland the pie is improved by the addition of other ingredients such as bacon, mushrooms, hard-boiled eggs, herbs and chicken stock. Some recipes use milk or cream instead of stock, and rump steak in place of the bacon.

Breast meat from 8 young rooks
8 rashers streaky bacon, chopped
225 g (8 oz) mushrooms, sliced
2 hard-boiled eggs, quartered
450 ml (¾ pt) chicken stock
1 tbsp fresh mixed herbs
Black pepper
225 g (8 oz) short crust pastry
1 egg, beaten

Pre-heat the oven to 200°C/400°F/gas mark 6

Soak the rook breasts in salted water for 24 hours. Rinse in cold water. Place the meat, bacon, mushrooms and hard-boiled eggs in a pie dish. Sprinkle with herbs and black pepper before adding the stock. Cover with the pastry, seal and decorate the edges. Make a hole in the centre of the pie and brush with beaten egg. Cook in a hot oven for 20 minutes. Brush again with the beaten egg then turn down the oven to 180°C/350°F/gas mark 4 and cook for another hour.

Battered Snipe

Serves 4 as a starter

Snipe breasts are deep fried in batter and served with a dip as a starter to a meal or amongst a selection of canapés for a drinks party.

Breast meat from 4 snipe
Oil for frying

For the batter
2 tbsp self-raising flour
2 tbsp milk
1 small egg

For the dip
2 tbsp crème frâiche
2 tbsp mayonnaise
1 tsp whole grain mustard

To make the batter, whisk the ingredients together until smooth. Leave to stand for 30 minutes. Mix together the ingredients for the dip. Coat the snipe breasts in the batter. Deep fry them four at a time in very hot oil until the batter is golden brown. This will take 3–4 minutes. Drain on kitchen paper. Serve on one large plate with the dip, garlic bread, cherry tomatoes and sticks of red pepper and courgette.

Super Snipe

Serves 2 as a starter

Snipe are fiddly birds to pluck so to save time just cut off the two snippets of meat from the breast bone.

Breast meat from 2 snipe
1 tbsp olive oil
Dash of lime juice
Dash of port
Salt and pepper
4 triangles buttered toast
Lime slices for garnish

Heat the oil in a frying pan and sauté the breasts for 2 minutes each side. Place each breast on a triangle of toast. Deglaze the pan with the lime juice and port and season with salt and pepper. Drizzle the pan juices over the snipe and serve at once as a super starter.

CHAPTER SEVEN

Hare

Leaper of Ditches...

A leaper of ditches, a cropper of corn,
a wee brown cow with a pair of leather horns.

Long ago in the dark days a wicked old woman lived in a cottage at the end of the lane. She was said to be a witch. It stood to reason that any lonely old person who lived alone, mumbled and had picked up enough knowledge in a lifetime to know about herbs and be able to cure simple ailments was sure to be suspect. Near her house stood an ancient orchard and in it lived a hare. Try as they might the locals could not bag it for it would make a fine meal. The hare seemed gifted with powers that saw her slip through the only unguarded gap in a hedge, dodge volleys of shot from their crazy old muzzle-loaders and avoid snares. She left the fleetest lurcher standing and all agreed she led a charmed life. It was a small leap of belief for unlettered locals to conclude that hare and witch were the same creature. You never saw them both at the same time and those who spied on the house swore that they had seen the old girl incanting and transforming before their very eyes before dashing out into the meadow to graze.

They may not have known much but they did know that the only way to destroy a witch was with a silver bullet. Bullion was in short supply in Lower Snodgrass on the Wold but the keeper had a waistcoat with silver buttons, a fugitive from the better wardrobe of a previous employer. He was persuaded to load one into his gun. Being the

113

best shot in the village he was hidden by a tempting gap and the locals lined out and drove the orchard towards him. Sure enough old puss came streaking through, ears laid back and the keeper swung through with deadly aim and fired. Boom of black powder, flash of orange flame and the silver bullet flew true. The hare rolled over with a hideous, unearthly scream. At that very moment the old woman's cottage burst into flames, the thatch was tinder dry in the hot weather, there was no chance of escape and she perished in the flames, shrieking piteously. The mighty Nimrods nodded their heads wisely. What more proof could you need?

The hare is deeply woven into the folklore and mythology of many civilisations and is a creature of magic and superstition. Should a hare cross your path it is a sign of bad luck, a belief held to this day even by educated people. In Christian countries it is an evil spirit but also a 'familiar', along with the cat, of the mother goddess to whom it was sacred. Scottish fishermen will not go to work if they see a hare on the way to the harbour. Even to use the word 'hare' was unlucky and if reference to it were unavoidable it would be to 'the furry creature with long ears'. Should a pregnant woman encounter a hare, her child was likely to be born with a hare lip. While haranguing her soldiers to defeat the Romans, Boudicca released a hare from the folds of her tunic. The way it ran and the direction it took would be omens for the battle. A hare or sometimes a cat often was buried in the foundations or under the hearth of ancient houses and churches to ward off evil spirits. A hare's foot in the pocket warded off bad luck and various ailments; the diarist Samuel Pepys carried one with him always. More practically a hare's foot made a fine brush used by goldsmiths to sweep up gold dust or by housewives to clean *objets d'art*.

No OTHER WILD ANIMAL HAS BEEN GIVEN SO MANY NAMES as the hare for it is a potent beast of ancient folklore, custom and superstition. As well as the widely used 'Puss', 'Old Sally' or 'Old Sarah', among those listed in a thirteenth-century Welsh book of venery are the following. The hare hunter was to recite this as a liturgy to bring him good fortune and to increase his power over his quarry.

The hare, the harekin
The Big-bum, Old Bouhart
The hare-long, the frisky one
Old Turpin, the fast traveller,
The way beater, the white spotted one,
The lurker in ditches, the filthy beast
Old Wimount, the coward,
The slink-away the nibbler
The one it's bad luck to meet, the white-livered,
The scuttler, the fellow in the dew,
The grass nibbler, old Goibert
The one who doesn't go straight home, the traitor,
The friendless one, the cat of the wood,
The starer with wide eyes, the cat who lurks in the broom,
The purblind one, the furze cat,
The clumsy one, the blear eyed one,
The wall eyed one, the looker to the side,
And also the hedge frisker,
The stag of the stubble, the springer,
The wild animal, the jumper,

The short animal, the lurker,
The swift-as-wind, the skulker,
The shagger, the squatter in the hedge,
The dew beater, the dew hopper,
The sitter in its form, the hopper in the grass,
The fidgety footed one, the sitter on the ground,
The light foot, the sitter in the bracken.
The stag of the cabbages, the cropper of herbage,
The low creeper, the sitter still,
The small-tail done, the one who turns to the hills,
The get up quickly,
The one who makes you shudder,
The white bellied one,
The one that takes refuge with the lambs,
The numbskull, the food mumbler,
The niggard, the flincher,
The one who makes people flee, the covenant breaker
The snuffler, the cropped head
His chief name is scoundrel,
The stag with the leathery horns,
The animal that dwells in the corn,
The animal that all men scorns,
The animal that no-one dare name...

The list goes on and it would take a hunter of good memory to recall them all on the morning of his expedition and some time to incant them. It is a long catalogue but some of the names are charming, mystical and expressive.

The hare has intrigued man for many centuries and features in religions. In ancient Egyptian art it appears as a hieroglyph with the meaning 'existence' and more pragmatically the ancient Egyptians kept hares in corrals for hunting. In China you referred not to 'The Man in the Moon' but to 'The Hare in the Moon'. The hare appears on Grecian and Roman pottery and crops up in European mythology. Archaeologists have found hare bones mixed with those of dinosaurs showing that such a creature existed long ago and survived whatever disaster wiped out their larger relatives: there could be no better example of the meek inheriting the earth. Legend has it that the hare is always female for the male or jack, being an impetuous chap, was the first to dash off the gangplank of Noah's ark and drowned leaving his wife bereaved. Myths about the sexuality of the hare abound.

It is a ruminant that grazes but does not chew the cud, another anomaly. It eats its food twice, chewing pellets of dung that contain half digested food. It is one of those creatures that lives its life in the open without shelter. Even deer sleep in thickets, badgers, rabbits and foxes have their holes but not the hare; she lives and dies alone out on a vast Suffolk ploughing, taking what the climate has to throw at her. She lays her young in forms apart from one another on the eggs-in-baskets principle, going round at night to suckle them. The leveret depends on its speckled fur and ability to lie stone still for its survival for they are often scragged by foxes. A leveret will emit a wild scream when threatened which makes the mother come running. She is a timorous beast but will see off a fox and even attack a human who touches one of her babies. Although she sleeps rough she will make a shallow scrape in the ground known as a form. This is deeper one end than the other and is worth studying for it is more than a simple trench. When the hare snuggles into it she faces the wind looking out for enemies with her back sheltered by a small parapet of earth. Many a ploughboy spotting a hare in the form has taken a shot at her with his rusty gun only to find her dashing off unhurt. You may see her but her earthwork is designed to protect her vitals.

As a mover she is another curiosity. She never walks but hops so when travelling slowly appears ungainly. Let her burst into a sprint which sometimes she does for the sheer joy of living and she is a different animal. Her long back legs are powerful and when pressed she runs uphill leaving enemies labouring in her tracks. However, she usually runs in a great circle ending up in the field where she was lifted so the canny spectators at beagling meets knew that if they stood their ground the hare would, sooner or later, return and they would see the sport while the younger keen ones were far away running hard. Hares like chasing things for fun and were known to race on a grass airfield in Northern Ireland called Aldergrove. Here the hares would line up like sprinters and wait for a plane to taxi prior to take off. They would sprint alongside until it rose into the air. It was said that one enterprising pilot in hungry times during the war arranged to taxi several times back and forth, drawing the hares towards a gap in the hedge where lurked his pal with a shotgun. She is a mighty leaper, frequently flying over wide dykes and swimming in salt creeks or fen drains. She was recorded once as leaping clean over a wall seven feet six inches high.

She had her favourite fields and her secrets were jealously guarded. An old farmer lay on his deathbed, his sons gathered round eager to learn the whereabouts of the family fortune. His last moments approached and he beckoned his eldest son to lend an ear. All craned forward to glean the accumulated wisdom of ninety years. Gathering his last breath the old man croaked, 'Dew yew allus look an oat stubble for a heer...' and with that he expired. Another old hare poacher would never reveal the secret of his success until he too was on his last legs. He used to fill his pockets with parsley seed and wander about on a stubble, appearing to look for mushrooms, but secretly scattering it here and there. When it germinated every hare from the parish came looking for it so he knew just where to set a snare. That secret was worth keeping for had it been common knowledge they would all have been at it.

Another old trick used the hare's habit of staring at an enemy from the safety of her form. It took two people, one to walk in front of the hare, not so close as to start her, but so that he drew her full attention. If on his own the man would flourish a spotted kerchief which he would leave hanging on a thistle. While the hare was gazing at the distraction, he or his mate walked up behind her and threw himself bodily upon her, pinning her to the ground. This was a well-known trick and no old wife's tale. She was easy to call by means of a hare pipe, an instrument that gave off a thin, reedy whistle such as you get by blowing on a grass blade. Some could do it by sucking wetly on the back of a hand. So deadly was a hare pipe that it was outlawed as early as the reign of Richard II, legislation reinforced later under Queen Anne. As recently as March 1910 two men were convicted of taking six hares by means of a pipe. Many could call hares and one of the most famous proponents of the art was the late Mackenzie 'Kenzie' Thorpe, the Lincolnshire wildfowler and poacher. He could produce a thin wailing cry with a sadly falling cadence that brought hares from anywhere within earshot. He skulked in a fen drain and bowled them over as they lolloped towards him. In one session he shot sixteen and had to carry them all home and as an average hare weighs in at seven pounds you will understand him when he says that he was, 'ver ver warm...'.

The brown hare, (there are three hares in the British Isles, the brown, the mountain and the Irish), remains a fair mark for the sporting gunner on condition he intends to eat her. She is wonderful on the table but it is a sin to shoot something you do not intend to eat. However, remember when you pull the trigger that you are shooting part of ancient mythology, a creature of magic, of the moon, symbol of the hearth, one who dances and frolics under the moon on lonely fields, one who escapes by running up hill, who can see better behind her than in front, who squeals like a baby when hurt, gnaws her own dung, and was worshipped by ancient peoples of whom we know little. It is a weighty responsibility.

The final words on this amazing animal we leave to Master William Twyti the huntsman to Uther Pendragon, father of King Arthur. Twyti spent his life pursuing great boars and stags and that was all his admirers wished to talk about. But get him onto the subject of hunting the hare and he would sparkle. He thumped his glass upon the table and discoursed on the marvels of this wondrous beast declaring that,

'...you could never blow a menee *for it because the same hare could at one time be male and another time female, while it carried grease and croteyed and gnawed, which things no beast on earth did except it.'*

I leave you with that thought.

Greyhounds in the Slips

The poaching 'moucher', as that wonderful country writer Richard Jefferies called him was useless without his long dog. The running dog was the chain that held a poaching gang together. Let the keeper destroy their dog by spear, poison or shot and the gang would disperse. A dog might be trained to ride snoozing on an old sack in a carrier's cart. Let the driver spot a hare in the form in a roadside field and he would call 'whoa' to his horse, make sure he was not observed before taking out his catapult with which he was a deadly shot. Poor 'puss' lay twitching and the dog slid like a shadow from its bed and over the park wall returning a moment later with the prize, the booty being concealed in some secret pace; a picture of innocence the carrier resumed his journey.

Should the keeper happen on the poacher and order him to call up his dog the rascal would whistle and shout his utmost but little did the keeper know that the dog had been trained to run home when it heard the command to, 'Come yew here...'. The long dog was of special value because a hare was large enough to keep a family going for

more than a week or she could be changed into coin of the realm for 'puss' was eminently marketable. Coursing became a recognised field sport, although its roots were ancient and went back to the Pharaohs. Its day came, flourished, and waned as public opinion shifted and the Hunting with Dogs legislation put an end to it. Unlike in fox hunting there was little room for compromise, no legal loophole to exploit and along with its curious and colourful adherents and iconic events such as the Waterloo Cup, hare coursing faded into oblivion.

The coursing flag had to be flown one last time before being struck for ever, so at the fifty-ninth minute of the eleventh hour, as a gesture of defiance I went to the ancient Cambridge and Isle of Ely Coursing Club's final meeting at Fulbourn in Cambridgeshire in order to watch the sun set on a sport enjoyed once by Royalty. The sad occasion was at Queen's Farm, owned by that fine country sportsman Mr John Lacey, where there was a strange cross-section of sporting humanity. There were 'cammo' jackets and tweeds; cut glass accents blended with the twang of the Midlands and the lilt of Pakistan; battered old vans rubbed muddy shoulders with Range Rovers. 'First course at 9 sharp', it said on the programme. Being used to martinets who run shooting days with a strict adherence to timings I was ready for the off, eager to savour every second of the last ever coursing meeting. An hour and a half later we shuffled down the cart track towards the eighty-acre stubble. They have had two hundred years to get themselves organised and even at their final meeting they could not get their act together; too late now. I thought of offering my services as a beater, as twenty quid and a bottle of beer are not to be sniffed at by a pensioner, but the team looked lean, mean and youthful with great boots, built for speed and endurance so I hung back. Anyway, I wanted to see the action.

I could have coped for they spent ages standing still or moving at snail's pace flapping plastic flags. The slipper seemed to my uneducated eye to give generous law. I was almost shouting at him to let go as the first strong hare came speeding through. On it went until it seemed it must escape and only then he slipped. This was the g-spot moment, the hair-crackling speed, like twin arrows from two bows the first two greyhounds, with arched backs and dirt spurting from their feet, streaked away. In no time they were up to the quarry and then the hare turned, turned again and jinked, (all this counts for points) until she decided she had toyed with them enough, then laid back her ears and finding second wind zipped away through the hedge and off. The dogs faded and slowed to a trot, tongues lolling, flanks heaving. The judge mounted on a big cob, raised the red kerchief and the cognoscenti marked their cards.

That was the pattern. We spectators wandered hither and thither not sure where we were supposed to be, passing gangs vaguely drifting the other way but somehow it hung together and muddled along. During the whole day I only saw one hare killed, a poor thing with matted coat and wasted muscles, better off culled. The idea is not to kill the hare. In all the meets in a season of the National Coursing Club only 126 hares were killed; more are shot on one drive on a hare shoot. The competitors were unanimous that the ban was disastrous news for hares as John Lacey preserves his hares for coursing. Would he do so any longer? How many landowners would shoot all their hares just to keep the poachers off their land? How many of those present that day would simply carry on beyond the law for there are no technical ways round the legislation?

The light faded, the spring sky grew dim and still they plugged away, miles behind on the card and in fact they did not get through it. It was typical of this delightful, old and faintly shambolic club and its sport that, as the sun set on them forever, they failed to complete their last day. Even at the end they were unable to change the habits of a century and, toiling good-heartedly but aimlessly, they shuffled off into oblivion. Typical of their generosity all the proceeds of the day went to medical charity. I watched the sport with open mind and concluded that it all seemed pretty harmless. It was a mean-spirited, spiteful, envious and destructive little law that had made criminals of those old boys, done harm to hares and denied the youngsters a future in their sport. What, I wonder, will happen to them now and to their long dogs?

Puss in Boots

S tanding in the famous gunsmiths, Gallyon's of Cambridge, one day long ago, a
man entered carrying a Wellington boot. He laid it on the counter and, with
an injured air, drew to our attention a peppering of tiny holes as in a colander.
This was, he claimed with indignation, a testimony to the safety standards at
the Suffolk hare shoot he had attended the day before. That old welly was an eloquent
spokesman for a sporting event now fallen from favour, once popular but renowned for
dodgy shooting and random pepperings.

Time was when poor puss was so numerous that she nibbled more than her share of
turnips, beet and young corn and her numbers had to be controlled. A poor excuse for
wholesale slaughter of such a mystical animal. But the hare has fallen on hard times and
the mass shoot has all but gone. It is no loss. The hare shoot was as much a social event
as a farming chore. Those who had a little shooting, farm workers, their families, guests
and amateur poachers assembled in the farmyard in the morning, exchanging greetings,
toting every type of gun from a crazy Belgian hammer job to 'Best' London. Enormous
boots were pulled on, wild-eyed dogs leaped from the back of trucks and dashed towards
the closest inanimate object before starting random fights. Heavy coats were dragged
on and, long after the advertised time of starting, a throng of about fifty armed men
assembled in the yard. The farmer, head keeper or the person set in charge of this motley
crew regarded them with apprehension.

Few in the assembly carry insurance or have experience of shooting in company of
more than two save for this one time a year, few are conversant with the safety rules of
the organised shoot, many are excitable, have few shots per season and should a half
chance present itself, will blaze away first and ask questions afterwards. Some have guns
which would give a safety officer nightmares – loose and ancient fowling pieces held
together with copper wire, some with loose hammers, an obscene blob doing duty as a
foresight, paper-thin barrel walls, one of them boasting a hole 'big enough for a warsp
to crawl threw' and some with woodscrews proud of the action where home repairs had
been made. Should a bystander be so unkind as to draw attention to some glaring defect
the proud owner of the weapon will respond with asperity and some indignation, 'Well,
it ain't never burst yit....'

The unfortunate shoot captain divides this disparate group into two teams trying to
keep old enemies apart and pals together, bearing in mind which drives are the hardest
walks and doing his best to save the older chaps from too much hard going. There is a

third special team of the really ancient and decrepit who are not expected to walk at all, there being no emergency services standing by. This half dozen are allocated a landrover into which they squeeze, often with guns already loaded. They will stand all day in the likeliest gaps and gateways for there is no point in growing old unless you grow crafty. Those who know them give them a wide berth. One who was weak and trembling either with St Vitus's dance or some ailment of old age quavered, 'I can't put the safety orf. Give it a shove for me....' I did so and beat a swift retreat for that safety catch would remain off until he fired. The other two teams clambered onto overloaded trailers clearly marked 'A' and 'B' breaking goodness knows how many Health and Safety laws. The day was under way.

The team to stand was dropped off along a long lane facing the rolling Suffolk downland, brown and striped with tender shoots of corn. The March wind was keen. The walkers lined out the best part of a mile away, for hare shoots took in vast tracts. On the word of command they set off in a ragged, wavy line, some striding boldly, others mindful of the tortoise and the hare, an appropriate fable given the occasion, paced themselves with an eye on a long day ahead. Boots picked up layers of mud until each man felt as though he had a hundredweight tied to each ankle. Then the lump would fall or be kicked off and he was fine for another hundred yards before it built up again.

Only a walking gun with little experience would shoot a hare as it dashed away as he would have to carry it all the way to the end of the drive across a thousand yards of heavy ploughing. This was the mistake of an eager youngster and a lesson learned the hard way. Really bad luck was to have a lively dog so that when your neighbour shot a walked-up hare the dog retrieved it and you ended up carrying it without even the dubious pleasure of shooting it. Walking guns left the hares well alone to lollop ahead, unaware of the danger as they criss-crossed on the skyline looking, as someone said, 'as big as donkeys'. In time one or two would tire of the game and, ears back, would streak for the gaps, gateways or holes in the hedge well known to them where they thought to escape.

It was here that the ragged army was deployed still as statues in the shade of ivy clad stumps. The heavy pellets pecked at the hares, tufts of 'fleck' or fur would fly, they staggered, rolled over and lay twitching sometimes crying piteously. Often they were missed and ran alarmed along the line so that if a man missed, his neighbour might score. The flat drill was dotted with fawn and white shapes of dead hares. At last the walkers toiled into view. Now came a final rush as hares dashed to safety, some breaking through and escaping to live and dance another day, many more rolling over. Some chose to run the gauntlet of the beaters and turned back seeking to break through rather than face the

terror ahead but now the walkers were close enough to home to take a shot or two.

With luck and a following wind there were few human casualties but it was in that final frenetic few minutes when hares were plenteous, dashing hither and thither and the field crowded that excitement ruled over prudence, that risks were taken. The hares were lugged by the back legs, bodies lolling, smashed limbs jiggling and slung onto a trailer provided. Then as on all shooting days came the post mortems, the casual mention of good shots, the compliments, commiserations and excitement until it was back to your trailer for the next drive. Hare shoots might produce five or six hundred hares in a day and while the event was not for the squeamish, that number was too many for the ground to support and there was risk of disease.

There are few hare shoots now and discerning sportsmen tend not to attend. Even on bird shoots where ground game is permitted there are few who will raise their gun to poor puss as, with ears laid back, she comes streaking through like a greased rocket. Although the humble man may have lost his sport, most people prefer it when the hare is left to gallop and frolic in the moonlight rather then end its life in a bloody pile in the back of a grain cart.

Recipes

Maybe the strange and unpredictable behaviour of the hare has resulted in the myths surrounding it. For centuries and throughout the world the mysterious hare has featured in legends and folklore often associated with the moon and fire. In Chinese mythology it was a symbol of resurrection, in India it was a sacrificial animal. Hares were sacred to ancient Britons and in the Middle Ages they were associated with fertility and witchcraft. Centuries ago hares were hunted with dogs to provide food. A recipe for hare cooked in ale with saffron appeared in the *Forme of Cury* published in 1378. In 1660 Robert May boned and baked hare in a pie seasoned with nutmeg and cloves and later in the eighteenth century jugged hare became a popular dish. A poached hare could be sold for a farm labourer's weekly wage. To buy the ingredients to make the strong meat palatable was beyond the means of country folk who preferred the sweeter tasting rabbit.

To roast a whole hare it should be young, wrapped in fat bacon and basted regularly to keep it moist. If roasting just the saddle of a young hare marinate it first in oil and spices and use the legs for stewing, soup or pâté. Alternatively remove the long fillets from the saddle, cut them in two, flatten with a rolling pin, season with black pepper and cook as you would beef steak. The Italians strip the meat from the front legs and cook it in stock with onions and herbs. They add raisins and pine nuts and make a sauce enriched with dark chocolate and balsamic vinegar. Old hares need slow braising in a casserole or the traditional jugged method.

A whole hare casseroled or cooked in a pie or pudding will serve six to eight people. The saddle will serve four.

Jugged Hare

Serves 6–8

Years ago a hare would be cooked in a large, brown, stone jug in a deep pan of water and simmered for hours on top of the kitchen range. The stew would be enriched with port, thickened with butter and flour and enriched with the hare's blood. This method may still be used using a large pudding bowl if you haven't a suitable jug. This recipe omits the blood but if you wish, just before serving mix it with a little flour and a tablespoon of red wine vinegar, stir it into the gravy and heat gently without boiling to prevent it curdling. Alternatively use your favourite casserole and cook the hare in a slow oven. Hare was often steeped in a pail of milk or cream to draw out the 'humours' before cooking.

1 hare, jointed
2 tbsp flour, seasoned with salt and pepper
2 tbsp oil
6 shallots, peeled and finely chopped
1 large onion stuck with 6 cloves
2 tsp fresh thyme
2 tsp fresh chopped parsley
Zest and juice of a lemon
¼ tsp ground mace
600 ml (1pt) game or beef stock
150 ml (1¼ pt) port
Redcurrant jelly
Forcemeat

110 g (4oz) breadcrumbs
25 g (1oz) shredded suet
1 tbsp chopped parsley
2 tsp thyme
1 large egg beaten
Salt and pepper

Pre-heat the oven to 150°C/300°F/gas mark 2 if using casserole method

Dust the hare joints with seasoned flour. Heat the oil in a large frying pan and brown the joints together with the shallots. Place in a jug or large pudding bowl. Add the onion, herbs, zest and juice of the lemon, mace, the stock and half of the port. Cover the jug or bowl with a lid of foil and place in a large saucepan half filled with boiling water. Simmer for 3 hours keeping the water topped up.

Alternatively cook in a casserole in a slow oven for 3 hours or until the meat is tender. Stir in the rest of the port and the redcurrant jelly and check the seasoning.

Mix together all the ingredients for the forcemeat and form into balls. Fry in oil or bake in the oven for 1 hour.

Serve with mashed potatoes to which have been added finely chopped leeks or chives, braised red cabbage and the forcemeat balls.

Spicy Saddle

Serves 4

A recipe for a baron of hare, which uses the saddle and hind legs appears in a gem of a little book given to me by Mike Eatley. *The Star Cookery Book No. 6* priced 2d, contains 500 cookery and household recipes (Metal Cleaning comes after Meat), published by the *Daily News*. There is no date but *The Star* was a daily evening paper first published in 1788 and subsequently taken over by *The Albion* in 1831. A herb stuffing was placed inside the hare, sewn up, larded all over and wrapped in well greased paper. It was then baked for half an hour in a brisk oven and served with green gooseberry sauce.

Saddle of a young hare
4 rashers streaky bacon
1 tbsp grated root ginger
3 tbsp crème fraîche
Port or red wine
Black pepper

For the Marinade
3 tbsp olive oil
2 tbsp chopped rosemary
2 cloves garlic, crushed
1 tsp ground nutmeg
1 tsp ground cloves
Black pepper

Pre-heat the oven to 180°C/350°F/gas mark 4

Combine the ingredients for the marinade, drizzle it over the meat and leave to marinate for 24 hours. Sprinkle the root ginger over the meat and lay the bacon rashers on top. Place in a roasting tin, cover with foil and bake for 1 hour or until the meat is tender. Transfer the saddle to a serving dish and keep warm.

Add the crème fraîche, a splash of port or red wine and black pepper to the tin and heat through gently. Remove the bacon rashers and carve the saddle lengthways parallel to the backbone in thin slices not forgetting the tender under-fillet.

Serve the sauce separately.

Somerset Hare

Serves 6–8

1 hare, jointed
450 ml (¾ pt) cider
450 g (1lb) cooking apples, peeled, cored and chopped
1 tbsp fresh chopped sage
150 ml (¼ pt) single cream
1 tbsp sage and cider jelly
Salt and pepper

Pre-heat the oven to 180°C/350°F/gas mark 4

Place the hare joints in a large flameproof casserole, pour over the cider and leave to marinate for 24 hours. Add the apples and sage, cover and cook for 2½ hours by which time the hare should be tender and the apples pulped. Stir in the cream and jelly, season with salt and pepper to taste and cook for a further 15 minutes.

Hodge's Hare

Serves 6

Leverets usually found their way into the kitchens of the big house leaving the older hares for the farm worker, often known as Hodge. A hotpot of hare would feed his family for several days. Unable to afford rich man's ingredients, to make his hare palatable he soaked the meat in salt and water rather than milk, used ale instead of port and vegetables and herbs from his garden. The hotpot was finished with layers of potato to make a whole meal in one dish. Alternatively top with short crust pastry to make a pie and serve with jacket potatoes.

Pre-heat the oven to 180°C/350°F/gas mark 4

1 hare, jointed
600 ml (1 pt) ale
2 bay leaves
2 sprigs rosemary
2 sprigs thyme
1 onion, thinly sliced
300 ml (½ pt) beef stock
1 tbsp flour
900 g (2lb) chopped mixed root vegetables (e.g. carrots, swede, parsnip)
Salt and pepper
900 g (2lb) potatoes
Knob of butter

Place the hare joints in a large bowl of cold salted water, cover and leave overnight. Next day rinse the joints and place in a large casserole. Add the ale, onions and herbs and leave to marinate for 24 hours. Blend the flour with the stock and add to the casserole along with the chopped root vegetables. Cover and cook for at least 2½ hours. Check for tenderness and add salt and pepper to taste. Boil the potatoes for 10 minutes, drain and cut into thick slices and arrange on top of the casserole. Dot with butter and cook uncovered for a further 30 minutes.

Potted Hare

Serves 6

This is a good way to use the front and hind legs left over from a saddle only recipe. It is easier to remove the meat from the bones after it has been cooked. The remaining stock may be used as a basis for soup.

Hind and front legs of one hare
1 onion, sliced
1 stick celery, chopped
2 cloves garlic, crushed
2 bay leaves
Zest and juice of ½ lemon
1 tbsp brandy
2 tbsp melted butter
1 tsp ground nutmeg
Salt and black pepper

Place the legs in a saucepan with the sliced onion, celery, bay leaves, garlic, salt and pepper. Cover with water, bring to the boil and simmer for 2½–3 hours or until the meat is tender and coming away from the bones. Leave to cool.

Remove the legs from the stock and strip off the meat from the bones. Pass the meat through a mincer or chop finely in a food processor. Transfer to a bowl, add the lemon zest and juice, brandy, 1 tablespoon melted butter and mix well. Add enough of the stock to make a smooth, firm mixture. Season with nutmeg, salt and pepper to taste. Spoon the paste into a dish, smooth the surface and seal with the rest of the melted butter. Chill for several hours before serving with oatcakes or crusty bread.

CHAPTER EIGHT

Rabbit

Bunny Rules OK

R abbits are notorious for breeding like – er – rabbits. Leave two of them alone for twelve months in perfect conditions with lots of carrots and you will have a million. In Victorian times the bunny was a valuable food source and sporting asset. A poor tenant farmer in Norfolk despaired at seeing his crops devastated by the grey army. If he touched so much as a whisker he would be out of his farm so, in the end, the poor man shot himself saying as he did so, 'I die, but the rabbits have killed me.' The rabbits may well have killed him but they kept thousands of others alive in hard times. So numerous were they and the meat so sought-after that The Rabbit Train ran weekly from Norfolk to London's Leadenhall Street game market. It was packed with thousands of rabbits all paunched and hanging neatly to feed the hungry masses in the Metropolis.

Wild rabbits were farmed on poor, sandy land and were more profitable than sheep or barley. Simpson wrote a book *The Wild Rabbit* (1895), on how to do it. An area was to be fenced, pipes and tunnels created, chopped turnips and carrots provided and breeding stock introduced, and then you just stood back and collected the money. The bunnies would have several litters a year and their babies or kits themselves were able to reproduce when a few weeks old. The farmer could also let a day's shooting on his warren for a tidy sum. He would keep the dead rabbits to sell so rabbit farming was an all round winner. In the villages many a peasant family was kept alive by fat-free rabbit meat containing no dreaded E number additives as the rabbits fed only on natural food. Sometimes they were the 'perk' of farm labourers – when the binder reduced the standing corn to a small square in which the rabbits were trapped the labourers waded in with sticks to bag themselves a dinner. A ploughboy would set a snare in a rabbit run in the hedge or he might own a mongrel capable of running down and snapping up a coney and, in earlier times, the yeoman had a goshawk specially for catching the 'small beast in hodden grey'.

Many birds and animals, as well as humans, eat rabbit – hawks, owls, foxes and badgers. The rabbit has many enemies and yet it is a survivor, as bullet-proof as Bugs Bunny in the cartoons. In the 1950s it was deemed such an agricultural pest that germ warfare was waged. A French scientist devised a deadly viral disease called myxomatosis, a cruel and dreadful scourge that killed a rabbit slowly so that it went blind and deaf, its joints swelled and it became a skin-covered skeleton. Passed on by the rabbit flea it spread like a forest fire. Some feared that the rabbit brought here by the Roman and reintroduced by the Norman, would become extinct. However, the little chap was resilient even to 'myxy' and the survivors changed their habits. They lived in smaller, scattered colonies instead of teeming warrens where the disease spread easily. They developed immunity to various strains of the virus and today the rabbit is back in business.

There are still old-timers who love rabbit pie on a cold evening with 'swimmers' (dumplings), carrots, onions and rich gravy, but 'myxy' put many folk off their rabbit pie and it is no longer a popular dish. There is cheap food in the shops and few people know how to skin a rabbit, let alone cook one.

Run Rabbit Run...

Go back half a century when farming would have been recognised by Turnip Townsend and Coke of Holkham. In my village they threshed with steam, ploughed with horses and ragged farm labourers in army coats, boots and waterproof capes went to work at seven in the morning on rusty bikes with their dockey bags on their backs. Dockey? It was an old East Anglian word for lunch, so called because in the hard old days you were not paid for lunch hour. A farmer would warn his men, 'Dew yew stop for lunch and I'll dock 'ee,' so 'dockey' it became.

In those days village people were expert at living off the land; money was short and there was no cheap supermarket food. You made do by tending a vegetable garden, keeping pigs and chickens, gathering hedge fruit and mushrooms, catching rabbits and fish, and doing a little poaching. The three mottos were: 'use it up', 'make it last' and 'wear it out'. There were no dustmen for there was never anything to throw away; ashes were put on the garden path and even empty tins were hammered flat to nail over rat holes in the shed. Everything else was burned, recycled or fed to the pig. Rabbits swarmed and kept rural communities going in hard times. Each cottager owned a rusty hammer gun, loose and potentially deadly but it was rare that one blew up. Some kept a hutch of ferrets or used long nets; ploughboys had their secret methods of bagging a rabbit should they spot a likely hole and even the vicar was a dab hand.

Once a year every able-bodied man in the village could join in and rabbiting became fun. This was at harvest time when the clacking binder started on the outside of a field and worked its way steadily into the middle, the square of standing corn growing smaller with each circuit, the thistly sheaves flicked out by metal fingers on the binder lying on the stubble waiting for the men to come round and build them into wigwams of 'shocks' or 'stooks'. Standing corn is beloved of rabbits – shelter from their enemies, plenty of food and easy living – until the machine comes and takes their world away. Bemused and disorientated they scuttle round the diminishing universe, seeking a way out but put off by the distance to the safety of the hedge. It would involve a long dash in the open and not many care to take the chance in daylight of running that gauntlet. They try the other side but again the clattering machine draws close and back they dash.

When the field had shrunk to the size of a large cottage garden the moment arrived – a time judged to a nicety by Harry 'Limes' Smith the tractor driver. As if by magic, people appeared: just happening to pass the gate and wandering in, children on their way home from school standing watching and, in what a minute before had been a deserted field, a score of people standing with their hands in their pockets. By the bush telegraph that served village communities, everyone knew when the cutting of the ten acres was reaching an interesting moment. But not all hands were in pockets; many toted a weapon, like a scene from the peasants' revolt. One hefted a pickaxe handle, another a cut-down haft of a hoe, a third menacingly clutched a walking stick and a fourth a dangerous looking hedge slasher.

Conscious that it was his hand that rested on the tiller of the events, 'Limes' brought his Fordson Major to a juddering halt where it stood gasping and steaming in the summer sun. He groped in the tractor toolbox and pulled out a long-handled hammer. He clambered down and strode into the remains of the standing crop, peering down like an old heron. This was the sign for the free-for-all. The bystanders rushed into the corn swinging their weapons peering round for the darting coneys. All kept a wary eye on the chap with the billhook for he knew not friend from foe but swung indiscriminately. Terrified rabbits darted this way and that, surprisingly hard to hit as they dodged and doubled. One or two bolder than the rest realised that it was wiser to face the uncertain dash across the open field than the horrors of the stamping boots and swinging sticks. They nipped out and darted between the fallen sheaves like rugby players until they reached the safety of the thorn hedge. One rabbit ran out but dived under the first sheaf lying on the stubble like an ostrich burying its head in the sand; that was its last mistake. The keen-eyed village postman had spotted it and winkled it out.

The rest might run but they could not hide. One by one they fell to stick, hammer or slasher. Some sportsmen were more successful than others; they were the calm ones who stood their ground waiting for the rabbits to come to them instead of thrashing about haphazardly. Their one swift stroke was usually enough and the rabbit lay limp. 'Limes' was one such, standing motionless, his deadly hammer swipe rarely missing. He had four rabbits while some had none. This was tough on the rabbit-less but Harry made no move to share his spoils among the less fortunate. What he had he was jolly well keeping.

That was great excitement for a quiet village after the war and slowly the crowd dispersed, strolling to where bicycles lay propped against the hedge. Rabbits swinging from the handlebars they toiled up Station Road homewards to the praise of their womenfolk. The wolf of hunger, never far from poor rural communities, had been kept at bay for another week and as so often, it was the rabbit wot done it.

Old Rabbity Tricks

The 'small beast in hodden grey' kept hunger away from many a poor man's cot in times past but it was also valued sporting quarry for the squire so his gamekeepers were anxious to keep it out of the workers' cooking pots. This was a running battle waged ever since the preservation of game along with the old argument about how anyone might be said to own a wild creature that came and went, crossing boundaries at will. Many a poor man had a hutch of ferrets and taking rabbits with them was as old as the Normans. A ferret would bolt a rabbit into the net, no noisy guns and, above all, no evidence as ferret and rabbit could be hidden in a loose coat pocket. The thing to avoid was a lay-up where a ferret killed the rabbit below ground. Digging was conspicuous and might be noticed so sometimes the ferreter would break off the beast's incisors with the hollow end of a key to prevent them from killing. Posh folk would buy a ferret muzzle, less brutal but the same effect. A big hob ferret might be 'lined', a cord attached to its collar so it could be traced if it stayed below ground.

Two Essex poachers were ferreting a steep bank. The ferrets were below ground and the rabbits were on the move. One chap suddenly found an unnetted hole under a grassy overhang. He had barely spotted it and was peering in when a rabbit shot out like a ball from a cannon, hit him straight between the eyes and knocked him over. He had two black eyes and a bloody nose but worse was to follow. Two keepers had seen the whole thing from behind the hedge. They emerged between guffaws of laughter and bagged them both.

Rabbits could be bolted in other ways such as the dodge where you set a lighted candle on the back of a tortoise. The tortoise entered the rabbit hole plodding downwards flat out at two yards an hour, the rabbits were scared witless and could not get out and into the net quickly enough. You could also make a concoction of sulphur that sent acrid smoke drifting through the warren and that too made the rabbits bolt. A simpler dodge was used by ploughboys and called for no ferret, no candle and certainly no tortoise – it needed nothing more complicated then a pile of old newspapers. Waiting for a fine night when the rabbits were far from the buries the lad would seek out the holes which he had spent daylight hours finding, sometimes marking each with a clean cut slice of white turnip the better to identify it in the dark. Into each he would stuff a ball of tightly rolled paper an arm's length down the hole. (He could use a lump of freshly cut turf but a keeper might see the marks where he had been digging.) Then he would run across the field frightening the coneys by trailing a cocoa tin full of small pebbles. The rabbits would dash back to the holes, try to go down, but were stopped short by the ball of paper. Their instinct was to stay still. The lad had but to thrust an arm down each blocked hole and pull out the rabbit. Stuffing both papers and rabbits into a sack he would slink away down the lane back to his mother and no one the wiser.

The two most popular tricks were the old-fashioned snare and the more complicated 'springe', a dodge that Shakespeare knew. The springe was a whippy hazel rod with a snare

on the end, bent into an arch with an ingenious pegging system to hold it under tension. This worked just as well for hares, pheasants, rats and surprisingly for woodcock. When the victim blundered through the wire it released the tension, the noose was snatched tight round its neck and the rabbit flicked into the air where it hung as by a hangman's noose. The only problem with this was that the dangling carcase could be seen from some distance and all knew that, '...thim owd keepers had eyes everywhere. Yew cain't get away wi' nawthen.'

Ploughmen made good rabbit catchers as they spent long, lonely days in the field gazing at the bottoms of two cart horses with ample time to spot holes in the bank. It was a simple matter to carry a pocket full of snares, not conspicuous unless you were searched, and set half a dozen as you plodded round, doing your mile of walking for your acre a day. Each time you passed you could check the snare and if it had caught, on the pretence of adjusting the harness, you 'whoa-ed' the horses, made sure the coast was clear and slipped to the hedge to bag the prize. It could be hidden under the grass safe from varmints until you slid it into your coat lining to take it home.

The old fashioned gin used to be a favourite but it was banned as being unselective and cruel. A poacher would skin an old doe, rub the inside of the skin with the earth and small droppings from a rabbit latrine and leave it as a draw. This would attract an old buck (always bigger and meatier), who would come hopping and sniffing along looking for love until, 'Click; there he was, ketched.'

For serious rabbit poaching you needed a long net and there are still a few experts who know how to make one and how to use it. The net was set along a rabbit field between the rabbits and their holes. You picked the right night and set it swiftly and silently. It was held up by a series of hazel pegs and was loose enough to bag slightly in the breeze. You needed a special dog trained to race round behind the rabbits, start them running but never chase one. Alternatively two poachers could trail a long rope between them sweeping the ground and startling the rabbits. The prey streaked towards the hedge and crashed into the net they could not see. They balled in the mesh and lay still. The netters worked systematically along the nets removing each rabbit breaking its neck and tossing it into a pile. They would be paunched and lugged away to a waiting carrier or stashed until it was safe to return for them. Millions of rabbits were captured in that way. Think of the families they fed and the Victorian and Edwardian heads warmed by beaver hats made from their skins.

Straddle Your Legs, Man...

If rabbits weren't so short behind
How many brilliant shots we'd find

There was a time when driven, walked up and bolted rabbits were a major part of sport with the shotgun. In the pre-myxy days they swarmed and some big bags were made. On 7 October 1898 five guns, all good shots, shot 6943 rabbits plus a few hares and partridges between 9.10 a.m. and 5.40p.m. This feat was achieved by keeping the rabbits from their warrens the night before so that they lay out 'rough' and could be driven home. Had the daylight lasted another hour all agreed that another five hundred might have been added. In 1861 in Leicestershire thirteen guns shot 3333 rabbits and twenty-six head of game; in North Wales in 1885 nine guns shot 5086 rabbits of which the Marquis of Ripon killed 920 to his own gun. If you really want to show off you will do as did Sir Victor Brooke shooting in his own park in County Fermanagh in 1885, who killed 740 rabbits to his own gun in a day. He fired exactly a thousand cartridges and shot from his right shoulder for one half of the day and his left for the other.

The rabbit shoot was a time of danger to bystanders. It was a noble Duke who cried to a beater, 'Straddle your legs man so I can shoot 'em as they run between.' Another Norfolk beater remarked admiringly at lunchtime. 'What a wunnerful shot the old measter be. Why he shot the very stick as I had in my hand, shot it in two and never touched me.' Another old chap wearing a smock emerged from the cover dabbing his nose with a spotted kerchief remarking, 'Oh Lor, Oh Lor, the old measter's got me agin....' A keeper approached the shoot captain, a noble Duke, touched his cap and murmured discreetly, 'Beg pardon Your Grace but you have wounded a boy.' 'What? What?' 'You have wounded a boy sir.' 'Absolute disgrace. Send him home immediately and tell him not to let me catch him out again today.' Those were the days when being shot by a member of the aristocracy was considered a compliment and an excellent jest combined, not to mention the compensation.

Myxamotosis wiped the rabbits from the face of the land. They returned but new shooters, not so well schooled, came into the field. They were more likely to shoot dangerously at hares and rabbits so the order now on most shoots is, 'No ground game', which would have puzzled the Victorians. Also beaters no longer care to be peppered and costly lawsuits might result. Rabbits are now shot at night from the backs of vehicles. They also fall to the ·22 rimfire rifle or powerful air gun and, while a minor diversion compared with the mountains of the slain of the 1860s, the little weapon provides interesting sport. Rabbit is as good to eat now as ever it was, truly wild meat full of flavour.

These days all good men go out pinging rabbits. 'Pinging' is the right word and I see it has been adopted by golfers to describe that sweet shot that clicks off the face of the club and flies to where you want it to go. 'Pinging' encapsulates the sweet shot from a ·22 when it hits the button and the rabbit tumbles to lie twitching. The very sound of the shot rings true like a perfectly timed cover drive or the flighted mallard that folds up like an envelope and thumps into the mud.

There are those who do their pinging from the back of a quad bike or a truck window. While that is fine for pest control or for shooting large numbers at night, your true pinger stalks on foot. You need little imagination to see yourself on the hill stalking red deer or creeping though a Wessex wood after a roe. The principles are the same: the silent approach, the use of the wind and keeping out of sight of quarry blessed with sharp eyes, ears and nose, the patience, the surgical precision of the shot and at the end of it something to eat. Thus a humble rabbit in the corn acquires the qualities of the 'Muckle Hart of Benmore' but the pinger gets to fire more shots and the bag is easier to carry home.

The best time for the itinerant pinger is on a warm evening when the corn is tall enough to hide a sitting rabbit except for its ears. The two furry fingers raised above the greenery have brought many a bunny to its doom. At this time the three-quarter grown rabbits born in early spring come on stream and they are the best to eat with the possible exception of a year-old one shot in dead of winter with a layer of fat along its fillets. The ·22 aimed properly damages no meat and anyone knows that a shotgunned rabbit is no fun to prepare or eat. A splinter of bone jammed between gum and tooth can dull the appetite. It is more pleasing to use a rapier than a battle-axe.

Thus I blew the dust off my ·22 BSA five shot bolt action and zeroed a clip at a 50-yard house brick, the target being rabbit size and you can see by the puff of red dust that you have hit it. The best shot for a rifle is to aim at the eye or the middle of the rib cage. In both cases a hit is deadly, no meat is damaged and, if you miss, you miss clean with little risk of a wounded beast escaping.

I left the truck by the bale stack and set off down the green tracks, peering through the gaps, easing along, a few steps and a stop, blending with the shadows. Swallows skimmed the green corn; there was a black cap in a thicket. Through a hole in the hedge a tell-tale pair of ears, pink and translucent protruded from the young wheat – a young chap. Leaning on the long stalking stick I slid the safety forward, lined up the scope on where his head ought to be and squeezed gently. There it was, the 'ping' shot, a meaty thwack and the bunny catapulted into the air and vanished in the green. I stood and watched awhile for where there is one there is often another for, innocent of the menace of the silenced hollow point, they do not always take alarm.

It lay as dead as last week and was paunched immediately. The great and wise Fred J. Taylor once wrote that a rabbit unpaunched for an hour became little better than carrion. I slipped him into the cavernous bag, wiped the knife and moved on, a shadowy but substantial shadow against the quickthorn.

Round the bend on the newly drilled game cover sat a full grown one out in the middle. This time it was the rib shot and he too sprang forward on impact and fell to lie scrabbling. Thus the last hour of daylight slipped by, a brown owl hooted in the oaks and cock pheasants crowed and whirred. A grey partridge chirruped and strings of rooks flew over, their day's feeding done.

The bag was heavy by the time I arrived back at the truck for it held six good rabbits, two long shots had clean missed and none was lost. Skinning young rabbits is child's play and in no time a jumble of joints with a little garlic, some red wine and beef dripping was spitting in the pan. Golden brown on the outside, slightly pink within and tender they were a feast for a true countryman or as they say, 'an honest man'. As he dragged the 'Muckle Hart' down the hill Charles St John could not have felt more at ease with life than the man who pushed the last of the picked bones to one side, heaved a sigh of contented repletion, raised a glass of the full-bodied red and drank not only to 'The Pinger' but to the humble rabbit.

Recipes

Central heating, cultivated apples and onions, pheasants, rabbits, herbs and spices were all introduced by the Romans when they invaded Britain in AD 43. Rabbits virtually died out after the Romans left and were not reintroduced until the Normans arrived when they were farmed for fur and food. The fur was fashionable and the flesh a delicacy. Farmed rabbit is tender and has a milder flavour than its additive-free wild cousin. It is healthy meat, high in protein and low in fat. Young wild rabbits may be brushed with oil and roasted, grilled or barbecued whereas fully-grown ones are best casseroled. Clean, netted rabbits free from shot are cook's favourites. Shot rabbits benefit from an overnight soak in salt water. Rabbit is as versatile as chicken. Ring the changes by adding more exotic ingredients from China, Mexico or the Mediterranean, or use local vegetables and dumplings for a warming winter meal.

The finest part of a wild rabbit is the couple of mouthfuls of tender strips found on the underside of the saddle. It would take a whole bag of rabbits to provide a main meal from such tiny scraps but they are worth collecting as, marinated and then briefly fried in butter, they are a treat. Serve on young spinach leaves for an unusual starter. Allow two fillets per person.

A good sized rabbit will feed 4 people.

Rabbit with Winter Vegetables and Rosemary Dumplings

Serves 4

It may just be a whiff of nostalgia but there are few things more welcoming on returning home on a cold winter evening than the aroma of a rabbit casserole simmering on the stove.

1 rabbit, jointed
1.2 litres (2 pts) chicken or game stock
1 thick slice wholemeal bread
Olive or rapeseed oil
225 g (8 oz) leeks, washed and sliced
225 g (8 oz) carrots, peeled and sliced
225 g (8 oz) parsnips, peeled and sliced
110 g (4 oz) mushrooms, sliced
Bunch of fresh herbs tied with string
Salt and black pepper

Dumplings
110 g (4 oz) self-raising flour
50 g (2 oz) suet
2 tsp fresh rosemary, finely chopped
Salt and pepper
Cold water to mix

Heat the stock in a saucepan then add the slice of bread and leave for 10 minutes to allow the bread to soften. Heat the oil in a large flameproof casserole and brown the rabbit joints. Beat the bread into the stock and pour over the rabbit. Add the sliced vegetables, bunch of herbs, salt and pepper. Cover, bring to the boil and simmer for 1½ hours.

Mix the dry ingredients for the dumplings and add enough water to make a firm dough. Divide into 8 dumplings and add to the casserole. Replace the lid and simmer for 20 minutes.

Serve with creamy mashed potatoes and Brussels sprouts.

Ginger Spice Rabbit

Serves 4

Pepper was the Roman cooks' favourite seasoning closely followed by ginger. As recently as 1970 Elizabeth David wrote that root ginger was hard to come by. Now it is available throughout the year and may be used to enhance many savoury and sweet dishes. Derived from the rhizome or root stem of the plant it freezes well and may be grated while frozen to 'ginger up' marinades, stir-fries and casseroles at any time.

1 rabbit, jointed
Oil for frying
1 onion, finely sliced
2 cloves of garlic, crushed
1 tbsp flour
300 ml (½ pt) dry ginger ale
300 ml (½ pt) chicken stock
1 tbsp root ginger, grated
1 tbsp wholegrain mustard
Salt and pepper

Heat the oil in a flameproof casserole. Brown the rabbit joints then remove them from the casserole. Fry the onion and garlic until soft, stir in the flour, add the ginger ale and stock and bring to the boil stirring all the time. Add the grated root ginger, wholegrain mustard, salt and pepper. Return the rabbit joints to the casserole, cover with a well-fitting lid and simmer on top of the stove for 2 hours or until the meat is tender. Adjust the seasoning if necessary.

Italian Rabbit

Serves 4

Rabbit is popular in Italy and there are many regional recipes. In the North they use red wine and tomatoes but the Sicilians favour *agrodolce* – sweet and sour, and use raisins, pine nuts, sugar and vinegar. Most Italian homes have basil growing in small pots and window boxes around the house and the sweet leaves are served in tomato salads, with mozzarella cheese, in stuffing, meat and egg dishes. Basil is the main ingredient of *pesto Genovese*, Liguria's most famous sauce. Bunches of leaves are pounded in a mortar and pestle with garlic, salt, pine nuts and pecorino cheese. Olive oil is slowly added to make a green paste. Red pesto also includes tomatoes and is a sweeter sauce. Italians are not especially fond of red meat preferring veal, duck and especially rabbit.

This recipe uses fennel, tomatoes, olives and ready-made pesto sauce.

Pre-heat the oven to 160°C/350°F/ Gas mark 4

Place the rabbit joints in a shallow dish. Mix the ingredients for the marinade and pour over the rabbit. Leave in the refrigerator for 24 hours.

Drain the meat and save the marinade. Heat the oil in a flameproof casserole and fry the rabbit joints. Add the marinade, chopped tomatoes, fennel, salt and pepper. Cover with a lid and cook in the oven for 1¼ hours or until the rabbit is tender. Stir in the pesto sauce and the olives and cook for a further ¼ hour.

Sprinkle with fresh basil leaves before serving.

1 rabbit, jointed
Olive oil for frying
400 g (14 oz) tin chopped tomatoes
1 bulb Florence fennel
1 tbsp green pesto sauce
12 black olives
Salt and pepper
Basil leaves for garnish

For the marinade
1 tbsp olive oil
2 tbsp white wine vinegar
3 tbsp chopped basil
1 shallot, finely chopped
2 cloves garlic, crushed
150 ml (¼ pt) white wine

144

Chilli Con Coney

Serves 4–6

The Romans called the rabbit *cuniculus*. From this word came the Italian *coniglio* and the English term *coney*. Originally from Mexico, chilli con carne is a hot fiery dish made with minced beef, onions, red kidney beans and spices. Any leftover game meat shredded or finely chopped in a food processor may be used instead of beef. Here the rabbit joints are cooked first making it easier to remove the meat from the bone. The cooking liquid is then reduced to make the stock.

1 rabbit, jointed
2 onions, finely chopped
1 carrot, chopped
2 sticks celery, chopped
Sprigs of thyme and rosemary
Bay leaf
Salt and pepper
Olive oil
400 g (14 oz) tin chopped tomatoes
150 ml (¼ pt) rabbit stock
2 cloves garlic, crushed
1 tbsp tomato purée
2 tsp chilli powder
1 tbsp fresh thyme
1 tsp sugar
Black pepper
420 g (15 oz) tin red kidney beans in chilli sauce

Place the rabbit joints, 1 chopped onion, carrot, celery, herbs, salt and pepper in a large saucepan. Add enough cold water to cover the meat, bring to the boil and simmer for 1–1½ hours until tender. Remove the joints and, when cool enough to handle, strip off the meat and cut into very small pieces or chop in a food processor. Reduce the stock and strain. Heat the oil in the pan and soften the second chopped onion. Add the meat then stir in the tomatoes, stock, crushed garlic, tomato purée, chilli powder, thyme, sugar and black pepper. Cover and

simmer for 30 minutes. Add the red kidney beans in chilli sauce and cook for a further 5 minutes.

Check the seasoning and serve with rice.

Rabbit Normande

Serves 4

It was the Normans who reintroduced the rabbit so it is not surprising that it has always been an important part of French cuisine. There are many variations of French mustard – yellow Dijon is made from black mustard seed with wine and spices. French tarragon has a subtle flavour and its name *estragon* is a derivative of the Latin *dracunulus* meaning little dragon.

1 young rabbit, jointed
Olive or rapeseed oil
225 g (8oz) mushrooms, sliced
1 dessert apple peeled, cored and chopped
1 tsp dried tarragon
150 ml (¼ pt) white wine
200ml crème fraîche or double cream
1 tbsp Dijon mustard
1 tbsp French wholegrain mustard
Salt and black pepper

Pre-heat the oven to 180°C/350°F/gas mark 4

Heat the oil in a flameproof casserole and brown the rabbit joints. Add the mushrooms, apple, tarragon, salt and pepper. Whisk together the cream, wine and mustards and pour over the rabbit. Bake for 1½ hours or until the meat is tender.

Serve with mashed potato and French beans.

CHAPTER NINE

Venison

The Muckle Hart

With Queen Victoria not long upon the throne, gentleman of leisure, Charles St John, followed the new fashion and sought recreation in the wilds of Scotland. Royal patronage encouraged it and Prince Albert's discovery of stalking and grouse shooting brought the glens and mountains within the ken of a new generation of sportsmen. Her Majesty wrote a journal of Royal holidays in the Highlands, prompting from razor witted Disraeli, the barbed compliment, 'We authors Maam...'.

St John had heard tell of a mighty stag known as the Muckle Hart of Benmore, said to lead a charmed life, unapproachable and protected by a bodyguard of lesser beasts to warn him of trouble. Many had tried and failed to bring him to the larder and St John allocated a few days of his sporting life to the challenge. He had little else to do. He set off on a Monday in the company of his reluctant manservant Donald who had no stomach for the expedition, muttering that, 'there are beasts as good closer to home – a feckless errand...', and the great deerhound Bran, hero of bloody tussles with deer and fox. They tramped the hill, saw several lesser beasts and, never happier than when pulling the trigger, St John bowled over a wild cat sneaking back to her lair at dawn. After a fruitless day they spent the night in a shepherd's hut eating freshly caught trout, oatcakes, milk and 'a modicum of whisky'. The shepherd had encouraging news for he told them the stag was in the area and he left a slot, 'like that of a good sized heifer'.

Next day they were off at dawn with Malcolm the shepherd accompanying them for some of the way. Breasting a slope two golden eagles rose heavy and gorged from the carcase of a sheep. Malcolm vowed revenge and they left him digging an ambush pit near the kill. Donald continued to grumble but towards afternoon staring at a boggy bit of ground, he let out a Gaelic exclamation. There was the slot of the largest deer any of them had ever seen. They followed the track for some distance until Donald who was glassing the far hill gave a grunt. 'Ugh; I'm thinking yon's him sir...' It was indeed 'him', only the tips of his antlers showing as he lay behind a knoll but he stood up and they could admire him in all his glory. It was an easy stalk of a mile and a half and the plan was for St John to stalk with the rifle and Donald to be sent with the double barrel to cut off the obvious line of escape, a pass leading down to the valley.

St John approached to within three hundred yards and could admire him all the better. 'What a noble beast, what a stretch of antler with a mane like a lion.' Suddenly he snorted alarm, three lesser stags previously unseen trotted towards him, alarmed him and all four dashed over the hill, shale tumbling down behind them. Donald had lifted the stags that dashed away and warned the nobler quarry. Another hundred yards and he would have been as good as in the larder. Donald returned cursing his misfortune in some colourful Gaelic oaths. They tramped their weary way back to Malcolm's shealing, made a bed by cutting bunches of heather, laying a plaid over them, more heather atop that and snuggling down. In a bed like that a man or a group of men could sleep in comfort on the coldest night.

• • •

THE NEXT MORNING AT DAWN our hero was out with Malcolm stumbling through the dark to the hole he had dug the day before for the eagles. It makes uncomfortable reading but this was the man who shot the last osprey in Scotland. He hunkered down in the hole and waited while ravens came and started to eat the carrion. I gloss over the distasteful scene where St John shoots both eagles in quick succession. Even he feels a moment of doubt at what he has done and sounds regretful but by then it was too late. 'I could not look upon the Royal birds without a pang...' The irony is that the sheep had almost certainly died of natural causes, but Malcolm was delighted. They spent the day fruitlessly scouring the high ground among ptarmigan – the only event of note was Bran killing an old, toothless dog fox after a short and one-sided chase. Night caught them still out on the mountain so they wrapped themselves in their plaids and slept soundly under the stars.

Next morning St John took a dip in the burn but Donald decided to keep dry. Food was short so St John shot a grouse sitting on a rock and when he went to pick it up found he also had killed its mate crouching behind it. They slogged on all day in rain with Donald growing more homesick by the hour. They were preparing for another night in the open when they stumbled upon an illegal still, complete with fiddler and drunken revellers dancing round an old barrel in a subterranean turf hovel. Donald cheered up immediately. 'It's all right enough sir; just follow the sound of the fiddle; it's that drunken devil Sandy Ross; ye'll never haud a fiddle frae him nor him frae a whisky still...' They waded a swollen stream waist deep holding their guns above their heads and were given a warm welcome. After a few drams of the fiery liquid Donald was capering round like a dervish.

Next morning it was obvious to anyone with half an eye that Donald was useless for action that day, snoring with his head in a heap of ashes. Tying Bran to his intrepid servant's belt so he would find him when he awoke, St John set off alone for the next day of his epic stalk. The weather had eased and in unfamiliar country the stalker explored some far corries for there were signs of deer having passed that way. He passed some stunning views, gazed over a lake covered with ducks and a lone heron and followed the feeder stream at the far end. To his great joy he found a slot of the Muckle Hart but light was fading. Using the heather and plaid method he made a bed and slept to dream of great stags thundering up rocky hillsides. Next morning he made sure of the hoof print, it was 'him' all right and shortly after, to his great joy, he spotted the stag lying down on a hillock on short grass but in an unapproachable position.

He backed off out of sight, found a burn and followed it round the hill until he could see the great beast again. He stood up to his knees in water spying until it rose, stretched like a bullock and went down to the stream to drink. 'You are mine at last,' he thought and bent down to prick out the nipple on his rifle and fit a new copper cap. Looking up the stag had gone, but as he was about to move rashly he saw where it was lying down again beyond the hillock. Lifting the rifle to his shoulder and gathering himself he kicked a small stone that splashed into the burn. The beast stood up in a moment. It was facing him and not the ideal angle for a shot but only fifty yards away and St John fired at the stag's throat.

He dropped to his knees but rose again and staggered up the hill. 'Oh for one hour of Bran,' thought the stalker, but that hero was safely tied up in the still far away. The stricken deer turned and made for the burn collapsing into it as though dead. Throwing down the rifle the stalker took his knife and went to bleed him but as he touched an antler it reared up and threw him violently down and stood over him with glaring, bloodshot eyes. St John rolled away but the animal charged and fortunately for him slipped on the stones and again fell, his great mane running with blood and water. St John took off his plaid and dashed it over the beast's head and rushed in for the kill, trying to stab it with his knife. A violent wrestling match ensued during which he nicked himself and wounded the stag in the leg before backing off at which the animal dashed away up the burn, limping with his fresh leg wound. He turned at bay, chest deep in the water, head lowered, panting heavily.

There was still a twist in the story for recovering his rifle and preparing to administer the *coup de grace* St John discovered to his horror that the bullets he had left were a size too big and would not fit the barrel. Nothing for it but to sit down and with his knife scrape one ball down to make it fit, 'an operation that seemed interminable'. Throughout the stag stood and glared at him. At last the ball was forced down the barrel and walking to within twenty yards he shot the Muckle Hart through the head. Wading in he floated him to the shore, sat down and checked his own wounds that were not serious save for one shin scraped from knee to ankle. The gralloch was done, the carcase stowed out of sight of scavengers and he set off to Malcolm's shealing with a light heart and, after delivering a suitable rebuke for his conduct the night before, had great pleasure in sending Donald back for the carcase, 'a duty which he performed before nightfall'.

Thus the story of the end of The Muckle Hart of Benmore, one of the finest stalking stories ever told.

Roe Morning

L ike the pageboy of Good King Wenceslas who walked in his master's steps for the heat of encouragement 'lay in the very sod, that the saint had printed'. I did the same, my saint came in the unlikely shape of the late Edgar James, head stalker on a great estate in Wiltshire. Edgar's every waking hour revolved round the deer. He did not care to take even one day off and entrust his ground to another. When forced to take a holiday he spent it moving a high seat, spying on his deer or doing a little stalking on his own account. It was his meat, drink, wife, child and all he needed in his life. The saints depicted in stained glass windows are thin bordering on the cadaverous but Edgar was a shambling bear of a man, slow-moving, bearded, rosy-cheeked, parsimonious of speech and deliberate. He lived his life in a loose-fitting camouflage jacket that possessed an aroma all its own; for all I knew he went to bed in it. I have seen Edgar's coat clear a path in a shop so that he could approach a crowded counter with a clear run. When that coat warmed up in a heated pub the bar would empty. He went through life believing that people were so polite they always made way for him.

Edgar once set his heart on finding a roe call of the sort used on the Continent but unavailable in the United Kingdom. It was a small pipe which gave off a thin whistle that at certain times of year could be a deadly lure. Edgar approached the toy counter of

a famous West Country shop, customers falling back respectfully when they caught a whiff of the coat. He rummaged among rubber dolls and teddy bears on display, pressing each one, listening to the squeak while shop staff looked on with alarm. He pounced on a rubber dinosaur, squeaked it and his face lit up. 'That's the one,' he said and laid down his money. He took his new purchase from the paper bag, whipped out an enormous skinning knife and, in a trice, disembowelled the dinosaur and removed the squeak. Leaving the wreckage and clutching his new treasure he stumped out of the shop just as the management were about to summon the men in white coats. That dinosaur squeak was responsible for the end of many roe and its makers would have been surprised to see to what use it had been put.

That was the man I followed closely that morning in May, the sun barely risen, the dew heavy on grass and cow parsley, the mist in the hollows, a dawn to gladden the spirit for it was to be a warm day. The dawn chorus was in full swing, a nightingale sang strongly from a thicket and blackbird, song thrush and a host of woodland birds carolled merrily. Pigeons cooed throatily, a turtledove crooned, cock pheasants shouted the odds and somewhere a grey partridge chirruped rustily. Overhead swifts, martins and swallows arrowed, catching the first flies of the day. Buds were bursting and, stand still for long enough, you could hear the soft rustle of things growing. I stared at Edgar's broad back and his famous coat, stained here and there with unmentionable substances, deer hair embedded in it and that special smell to which I had become inured. For a burly man Edgar moved like a cat, soft-footed and never a twig cracked underfoot. Two slow steps forward, a pause and the battered binoculars were raised slowly and he scanned ahead of him. When he stopped, I stopped and also scanned but in all our outings together I never spotted a beast unless he had spotted it first. How I longed to beat him to the draw just once.

When we saw a deer Edgar would tap me gently with his stalking stick and indicate a place somewhere in front and there was the red summer coat of an unsuspecting roe, usually a doe, feeding unconcernedly by the bushes. Her tongue wetted her black nose as she tested the breeze for scent, never relaxing but after each few mouthfuls raising her head and staring round. Her great ears rotated like radar dishes, pausing to catch something unfamiliar, changing direction, taking in every sound of the forest, identifying and dismissing each as non-threatening. Her world was full of enemies and she survived by keeping her eyes, nose and ears open.

Edgar spent many minutes glassing the animal for he recognised most of the roe on his patch. Stalking to him was not the modern style of deer 'control' which he described

152

bitterly as, 'You go out, you see a deer, you control it.' A good stalker spends a season studying his beasts, he learns what is the surplus of yearlings and does, which bucks are passing their prime and may be taken and which must be left so that at the end of his lease the deer are in a better state than when he arrived, and not damaging crops and trees. That is good deer management in Edgar's book but it could be frustrating for his stalking companion for he might spot fifteen deer in one morning but not one of them shootable. Many of them seemed eligible but Edgar knew better.

Thus it was that for many mornings I followed Edgar, stopping when he stopped, glassing when he glassed and learning about the roe. Rarely was I allowed to take a shot. On this morning he stopped as usual and spent an inordinate time watching a beast that stood half seen amongst the beech trunks. He studied minutely the yearling buck with little antlers, he examined the background making sure it was safe for a shot and he worked out the range, taking everything into account. This yearling was fraying trees and annoying the resident older buck and was ripe for the cull. At last Edgar indicated the animal and whispered, 'Shoot that one.' Now the moment of cold surgical precision, no room for a poor shot with such a stern taskmaster looking on.

Taking no chances Edgar held his stalking stick vertical, using his fist to make a rest. Leaning the barrel on his mittened hand I squinted down the scope, lined up the heart, no problem after practice at the cut-out deer in Edgar's paddock, took a deep breath and squeezed the trigger of the ·308. Edgar did not believe in going lightly armed for the worst thing in his life was a wounded beast that might take all day to find. The rifle boomed, the gases formed a puff of mist, eyes blinked and when they reopened the deer was gone. Not a miss surely. Edgar said nothing but stood still and glassed some more. He placed a finger to his lips and we waited; a wounded beast might spring up and run fuelled by adrenaline should we go rushing in. After an agony of waiting, with his standard, measured tread Edgar approached the spot and in a slight hollow lay the little buck, a frond of grass gripped between his teeth. The grape bloom of the eye was dimmed but Edgar did the old stalker's test of death by touching a grass stem gently on the eyeball. This would cause a reaction that no living thing could resist. There was none, the shot had flown true.

Edgar completed the gralloch with the practised hand of half a century and I was allowed to drag my trophy out of the wood to the waiting van. The sun was now above the rim of the beeches and less privileged people were getting up and going about their daily business. Back in Edgar's cottage he produced from a polythene bag the pluck, the liver, kidneys and heart. He sliced the meat razor thin and fried it lightly in dripping with eggs from his own hens and home-cured, smoky bacon. That was forty years ago and I can taste that breakfast as I write for it was one of the best I have eaten before or since. 'Stalker's perks' they called it and I wonder when I will eat another like it.

Having stalked with the best I realised what a commitment it would mean to take up the sport for myself. You needed the rifle, the land, the expertise, the patience and a special slant on life to become a stalker and there was not enough room in my world for any more passions. The sport was better off without me but I had savoured magic moments, walked in the footsteps of a giant and learned much of a fascinating field-craft. As for my little buck, his baby antlers hang on the wall as I write and glancing at them reminds me of happy days with a genuine expert and of the finest breakfasts an honest hunter could ever eat.

The Toothpick Deer

Most introduced species, brought here and released with the best of intentions, end up as disasters. Rabbits, pheasants and red-legged partridges we can live with but Canada geese, coypu, American mink, grey squirrels, zander, little owls, Japanese knotweed – the list of disasters is a long one and it would be hard to find a naturalist who would be sorry to see them go back whence they came. Another is the little muntjac, smallest of our deer brought over as an ornament, probably by one of the Dukes of Bedford who specialised in an ill-conceived introduction of exotics. The Reeves muntjac came from India where it was the natural prey of the leopard and tiger of which there is a shortage in Bedfordshire. There was nothing to control its numbers and as, in any month of the year, a female muntjac could be suckling a fawn whilst pregnant with the next; they bred like rabbits. The only predator of any significance was a prowling fox stumbling on a fawn left to crouch in the bracken awaiting its mother. A fair number were knocked over on the roads but apart from that everything in the muntjac's life was rosy. Plenty of food, good shelter, an agreeable climate and no real enemies made life in the United Kingdom closer to paradise than it was in the Indian jungles.

The small deer was just right for poor man's stalking for it had not lost the healthy respect for man, was secretive and as wary as any stag on the hill. Like the roe it called for an early rise, the creeping down sunlit rides, the glassing, the study of the animal and the accurate shot with a good rifle. A ·222 was the perfect weapon for this little chap but laws governing rifles for deer were brought out before such little creatures or even roe became a fair mark with the result that most muntjac stalkers went over-gunned. My keeper friend Ken Siford is a distinguished keeper in Hampshire but when first I knew him in Bedfordshire he invited me to shoot my first muntjac. We tested the rifle and I was mustard on the cardboard cut-out, having never heard of buck fever. As with my roe stalking with Edgar we set off on a magical summer dawn full of birdsong and what Wilfred Scawen Blunt in his lovely poem The Old Squire called, 'the pheasants and feeding things of the unsuspicious morn…'

Ken was an easier going tutor than my stalking friend Edgar James. He covered more ground and was more relaxed. We settled down to wait by some tumbled bales at a spot where he knew a good buck passed every morning on its way from somebody's garden where it lived to the feeding fields. Muntjac are fond of gardens where they can live for years in the shrubbery without being detected. The householder is puzzled by what eats his roses to the ground, decimates his vegetables and nibbles his precious bulbs. Our little buck was on time for Ken does his homework. Daintily he stepped across the meadow in which we hid. I checked the rifle and got a good lean on a firm straw bale and levelled at his chest. 'Wait until he stops,' hissed Ken. I was going to anyway and was lining up the shot. The deer had no intention of stopping but came forward steadily until Ken gave a short, sharp whistle. The buck stopped as though electrocuted and stared forward, wet tongue licking his nose to gather scent.

I lined up the cross hairs and suddenly I was trembling. The more I aimed the unsteadier I grew. He was not going to stand still forever and that put more pressure on me to make the shot. Now I was wobbling uncontrollably and where an experienced stalker would have lowered the rifle and taken a deep breath, the harder I tried to calm down the more I failed. In the end I fired a shot that went nowhere near the deer. The sound echoed and rolled along the hedges and was swallowed up in the woods. The deer looked round unable to tell whence the sound had come but showed no alarm.

Ken saw how things were and told me to lower the rifle and take a deep breath; the buck walked another twenty yards and stopped to stare round. For a second time I took the rifle, my knees turned to jelly, and again a shot of all of twenty-five yards went wide of the mark; better a clean miss than a wound. Finally the buck realised that all was not well and scuttled off towards a solid wall of bramble on the wood side and ran through it as though it were mist. Not for nothing is the muntjac known as the 'ridge-faced deer' for it can run through impenetrable cover. My embarrassment was agonising and apologies heartfelt but I had been in the grip of strong emotions. Since that day I have shot numerous roe and several wild boar and remained as calm as a surgeon with never a hint of a wobble and never a wounded beast. Just that once I wished the earth would open and swallow me up and now I know first hand what 'buck fever' means.

That evening Ken put me up in a high seat on the edge of the wood covering a ride where deer walked in the evening. I was to shoot nothing save a muntjac and he departed leaving me to my thoughts. The morning's disaster still rankled and I aimed in turn at various logs, tufts of grass and small birds finding myself rock steady and ice cool.

The man in the high seat sees the world go past, and roe and fallow plus a mangy fox passed below me. The fox should have been shot but I followed my instructions. At dusk he was there, one minute nothing, the next a handsome little buck browsing on the brambles that fringed the ride. I waited some minutes for him to turn broadside, took steady aim and fired my single shot. He flinched, and stiffened, his little tail stood out quivering like a bottlebrush, he took two faltering steps and dropped to the ground, twitched and lay still. Remembering Edgar's rule about leaving a shot deer before approaching I waited quarter of an hour and in near darkness climbed down, walked to the spot and there lay my first and last muntjac perfectly shot through the heart. Buck fever? What's that? The final treat was to take it home and eat it, the fact that I had bagged it making it taste all the better and to this day I contemplate his toothpick antlers with pride.

Before stalking and I parted company for good I added a sika to my list of victims. The sika is another import and a mixed blessing for it cross breeds with the native red deer with unsatisfactory results and a pollution of the pure bloodlines. It was all right when confined to Brownsea Island off the Dorset coast where it was introduced but a fire caused the deer to swim to the mainland to escape. Thence they spread north and colonised.

Stalking in the steps of Edgar James one bright morning we rounded a corner of the wood and about a hundred and twenty yards off stood a sika staring back at us. We froze and, after a long, hard look it resumed grazing. There was no suitable lean so Edgar indicated that I lie down on the spot. When the deer was preoccupied with feeding I eased myself down and lay luxuriously in a deep, moss-lined puddle in an old wheeling. Edgar did not encourage softness if it got in the way of a shot. To be fair to him he too lay down in it and an odd sight we must have made; two old buffaloes in a wallow.

The stag got wind of trouble and stared back over his shoulder and then moved slightly to quarter on. This was as good a chance as I would get and Edgar clenched his fist and plonked it in the puddle for me to use as a rest. I lined up the shot but it was poor visibility with a bad view of the vital chest area. Getting as much of it as I could in the scope I took a deep breath and, steady as you like, squeezed the trigger of Edgar's ·308. As with my roebuck there was a squirt of gasses and spray and I blinked, looked again and the deer was gone. I felt no confidence in the shot and neither, I suspect, did Edgar.

We rose, dripping, from our watery couch and plodded to the spot, still daring to hope, looking for 'pins and paint' to indicate a hit and there, ten yards further than we thought, lay a handsome sika stag fitting exactly in the very wheeling in which further back we had lain. I had aimed at the chest but the bullet had gone precisely through the thick of the neck and killed him instantly. I pretended that this was my intention Edgar offered congratulations although there was a hint of suspicion in his wise old eye.

Recipes

The growing interest in stalking, the increase of farmed venison and its appearance on supermarket shelves combined with endorsement from celebrity chefs has boosted the popularity of this well-flavoured meat, low in fat, versatile and available throughout the year. What makes venison desirable, whether wild or farmed, is that it is efficient at converting leaves, shoots and grass, not to mention carrots, potatoes and apples into lean meat.

The juicy saddle is the finest roasting joint. Two prime fillets may be cut from the underside of the saddle and the top may be boned to produce two superb strips of meat for flash frying. Alternatively it may be cut into juicy chops for grilling. The haunch and shoulder are also excellent roasting joints. Steaks cut from the upper part of the haunch may be grilled, fried or barbecued. A haunch or saddle of venison makes an excellent alternative to turkey or goose at Christmas – serve with red cabbage, chestnuts and cranberry relish for a festive touch.

Thinly sliced venison with chopped ginger, spring onions, cashew nuts and soy sauce makes an instant Chinese stir-fry.

In summer sausages, veniburgers, steaks and spare ribs make perfect barbecue fare. Brush steaks with oil, season with black pepper and cook on a hot barbecue. Coat finger-licking ribs with honey and a hot barbecue sauce and cook until brown and crisp. Marinate cubes of tender venison in red wine, olive oil and chilli powder or piri piri sauce to make tasty kebabs with any assortment of colourful peppers, fennel, onion, mushrooms, dried apple or apricot.

For warming winter casseroles the lean stewing meat is perfect for slow cooking with a variety of vegetables and spices.

Leftovers from a roast haunch or saddle can be rehashed as you would beef or lamb. Use any pink meat spread with fruit chutney in rolls or sandwiches for a packed lunch or picnic. Toss salad leaves and thin slices of cooked venison in a mustard and dill dressing for a light lunch or starter. For a more substantial and colourful lunch or supper add slices of mozzarella, avocado and tomatoes. Minced cold venison makes an excellent 'shepherd's pie' topped with creamy mashed potato, curry or chilli con carne with rice, or an Italian sauce to serve with pasta.

Humphreys' Haunch

Serves 10

The Romans served venison with dates, damsons and fruit sauces. According to Gervase Markham writing in 1660, roast venison should be studded with cloves and served with a sauce spiced with cinnamon and ginger, possibly to soften the strong flavour. This is not a problem in the twenty-first century but a little garlic, rosemary and mustard will enhance rather than mask the flavour.

Although a matter of taste roast venison is best cooked so that it is just pink in the middle. This way there will be enough outer slices for those who prefer their meat well done. Increase the cooking time to 20 minutes per 450 g (1lb) plus 20 minutes if you prefer the whole joint well done. If in doubt cook it as you would roast lamb. A haunch of fallow will serve 10 people, a roe haunch 6–8 and a muntjac haunch is enough for 4.

Haunch of fallow deer about 2kg (4–5lb)
Olive oil
3 cloves garlic, thinly sliced
2 sprigs rosemary broken into small florets
1 tbsp wholegrain mustard
Large glass red wine
1 orange, quartered
Black pepper
Quince or cranberry jelly

Pre-heat the oven to 200°C/400°F/gas mark 6

Rub the oil all over the whole joint. Make slits in the meat with a sharp knife and place a sliver of garlic and a floret of rosemary into each one. Spread the wholegrain mustard on the meat and sprinkle liberally with freshly ground black pepper. Place the joint in a roasting tin, add the wine and the orange quarters and seal with a sheet of foil. Cook in a hot oven for 15 minutes per 450 g (1lb) plus 20 minutes. Remove the foil for the last 15 minutes and rest the meat for a further 20 minutes. Serve with fruit jelly or whole grain mustard.

Spiced Venison

Serves 4

110 g (4oz) ready-to-eat prunes
450 ml (¾ pt) stock
700 g (1½ lb) boned venison from shoulder or neck
1 tbsp flour
3 tbsp oil
1 large red onion, sliced
110 g (4oz) mushrooms, sliced
2 cloves garlic, crushed
1 tsp chilli powder
1 tsp ground cumin
1 tsp ground cinnamon
150 ml (¼ pt) red wine
1 tbsp soy sauce
1 tbsp redcurrant jelly
Salt and black pepper
Fresh coriander leaves to garnish

Pre-heat the oven to 180°C/350°F/gas mark 4

Soak the prunes in the stock for 2–3 hours.

Put the flour in a bowl, add the cubed venison and stir to coat it all over with the flour. Heat 2 tablespoons of oil in a flameproof casserole and brown the onions. Add the mushrooms and garlic and fry for 2–3 minutes. Remove the fried onions, mushrooms and garlic and keep on a plate. Drain the stock from the prunes. Add the rest of the oil to the casserole and brown the floured meat. Stir in the spices and any remaining flour from the bowl. Return the onions, mushrooms and garlic to the casserole and stir in the stock, wine, soy sauce, redcurrant jelly, salt and black pepper. Cover and cook the oven for 1¾ hours. Stir in the prunes, check the seasoning and cook for another ¼ hour.

Stalker's Perk

Serves 2

The liver and kidneys of a yearling roebuck are traditionally claimed by the stalker to be eaten for breakfast on returning home. This will feed two hungry stalkers.

Fresh liver and kidneys of a yearling roebuck
225 g (8oz) mushrooms, sliced
4 rashers of bacon
Oil for frying
4 eggs

Wash and dry the liver and kidneys. Cut the kidneys in half and the liver into thin slices. Heat the oil in a frying pan and cook the bacon and mushrooms. Add the liver and kidneys and cook for about a minute on each side so that they are still pink in the middle. Keep the bacon, mushrooms, liver and kidneys warm in the oven and then fry the eggs. Serve on hot plates.

Venison Terrine

Serves 4

As well as the main ingredient of a stalker's breakfast, venison liver makes excellent pâté and terrines. Venison sausages are available from most butchers and supermarkets.

225 g (8oz) venison sausages
225 g (8oz) roe liver
6 rashers streaky bacon
1 tbsp red wine
1 small onion, very finely chopped
1 tsp dried thyme
1 clove garlic, crushed
Pinch nutmeg
Salt and black pepper

Pre-heat the oven to 160°C/325°F/gas mark 3

Remove the skin from the sausages. Chop the liver and bacon into small pieces. Mix well with the sausage meat, wine, onion, thyme, crushed garlic, nutmeg, salt and pepper. Turn into a well-greased loaf tin and cover with foil. Bake in the oven for 2–2½ hours.

Allow to cool and chill before slicing.

Venison Sausage and Mash Pie

Serves 4–6

This is a different way to serve traditional bangers and mash. There is a little more preparation involved but, as it is served in one dish straight from the oven to the table, it makes an ideal shoot supper.

2 tbsp oil
2 dessert apples, peeled and chopped
1 red onion, peeled and chopped
900 g (2 lb) venison sausages, skinned
2 tsp mild mustard
1 tbsp flour
1 tsp each fresh thyme and sage
600 ml (1pt) stock
450 g (1lb) potatoes and
225 g (½ lb) parsnips cooked together
Milk
Nutmeg
Salt and black pepper
Chopped chives for garnish

Pre-heat the oven to 180°C/350°F/gas mark 4

Heat the oil in a frying pan and soften the chopped apple and onion. Add the sausage meat to the pan breaking it up with a fork. Stir in the mustard, flour, and herbs. Gradually add the stock and simmer gently for 15 minutes, stirring occasionally to prevent sticking. Transfer to an ovenproof dish.

Top the mixture with the potatoes and parsnips mashed together with milk, salt, pepper and a pinch of nutmeg. Cook in the oven for 25 minutes or until the topping has browned.

Sprinkle with chopped chives and serve with a green vegetable.

Venison with Peppers

Serves 4

This colourful recipe was originally for hand of pork and has been a favourite for thirty-five years and passed on to many friends. It works really well with venison and is ideal for entertaining or a shoot supper as it may be cooked in advance and reheated when needed. The boned shoulder of a fallow deer gives about 675 g (1½ pounds) of meat.

700 g (1½ lb) stewing venison, cut into cubes
Rapeseed or olive oil
1 onion, finely chopped
1 tbsp flour
1 tsp Cajun seasoning
Salt and pepper
4 heaped tsps beef granules
300 ml (½ pt) hot water
400 g (14 oz) tin apricots in light syrup
1 tbsp tomato purée
1 tbsp soy sauce
1 tbsp balsamic vinegar
1 green pepper, deseeded and sliced
1 red pepper, deseeded and sliced
Flat leaf parsley to garnish

Heat the oil in a large flameproof casserole and soften the onion. Toss the meat in the flour together with the Cajun seasoning, salt and pepper then fry in the casserole until brown all over. Dissolve the beef granules in the water and stir into the casserole together with the juice from the apricots, tomato purée, soy sauce and balsamic vinegar. Add the sliced peppers, mix well and slowly bring to the boil. Simmer on a low heat for 1 hour or until the meat is tender. Add the apricots, check the seasoning and cook for another 10 minutes.

Garnish with chopped flat leaf parsley and serve with baked potatoes rubbed with sesame seed oil and sprinkled with sea salt.

CHAPTER TEN

Trout and Salmon

Tweed Silver

We made the long trek North in one of our regular torrential 'droughts' but when we got home a week later hailstones beat a tattoo on the road and my pond was overflowing. My keeper friend remarked, 'This is the wettest drought I can remember.' One chap flaunted the hosepipe ban by siphoning floodwater out of his cellar. Ordinary folk are kept in the dark like mushrooms but the official state of 'drought' did seem curious when it rained every day in May; it is humbling and shows how little we know. My neighbour had just been to Scotland for ten days but he was lucky for it rained only twice, once for four days and once for six.

The Tweed valley looked sumptuous in late May finery but the water was high, the colour of Darjeeling with twigs in it. The old saying is 'More water, more fish', but the little dears must be able to see your lure in the murk. Some cynic remarked that salmon fishing is like a blind man on a dark night seeking a black cat in a shuttered room – and the cat is not even there. I had three days on that famous river and had invited the odd chum to drop in for a cast or two. The beat lies above the magnificent bridge at Coldstream on the border between Scotland and England where the Scots crossed the river going north after their disaster at Flodden just down the road. The fishing is run like clockwork by head boatman Brendan Lough and his deputy Kevin 'The Hat' Wright. If there is a salmon on the beat they will not rest until it is found and anyone lucky enough to fish there has been with two of the best boatmen on the river. They are boatmen and not ghillies. A ghillie is one who reclines on a grassy bank puffing a pipe while the angler flogs away. Now and then he rouses himself to net a fish or advises to, 'Cast a wee bit closer to yon rock...'. The boatman spends his day at the oars holding a boat in a strong current, seeing to it that the flies work the lies and that the angler is doing it right. Any fish are credited to the boatman not the angler.

At the fishing hut Brendan's two dogs romped, tackle was assembled, coffee drunk, flies selected and plans made while in front rolled the magnificent Tweed as it has rolled for a million years. Number One son David went to fish on his own from the bank opposite the great monument looming high above in Coldstream High Street and I went with Brendan in the boat.

I started at a famous pool called the Duddo at the top of the beat. Here the water is swift, deep and turbulent. It would not do to fall in. I flogged it with the fly, Brendan inching the boat through the lies, pointing out underwater ledges and boulders behind which a fish might rest. The surface gave away the secrets of what lay below, a riffle indicating a ledge or a horse's collar wave revealing the hidden boulder. Salmon like to rest in easy water and those are the places to search out. No luck with the fly so we changed to the chuck-and-chance-it of the spinner, flicking it across and winding in slowly, feeling the thrum of the bait as it limped past hidden boulders. The spaniels sprawled in the bow watched every movement of the Blair spoon.

The black cat in the dark room was not there – notice that: not 'failing to take' nor 'being fished for badly', but just, 'not there'. Were he present he would be flapping on the bank in the face of such skilled angling. Fishless we tramped the riverside path back to the hut for lunch and there on the grass in the shadow under the picnic table lay an ingot of quicksilver with a smiling David sitting hard by. Fishing from the bank he had hooked, played and landed a hard fighting fish all on his own apart from an admiring audience on the town footpath. Having returned all his fish this season he was allowed to keep this one, the policy being catch and release with discretion. Lunch was a jolly affair and it was good that the ladies, grandchildren and family dog joined us in the sunshine.

In the afternoon we changed beats but this scribe was wearing the wrong aftershave for nary a nibble despite thrashing the water to a foam. Back at teatime with aching arms and a bad back I found my afternoon guest, David Wilson, slumped at the picnic

table, a broken man with a face like a bag of spanners and a tear in his eye. What could have happened? Bit by bit the tale was blurted out. He had hooked a fine salmon by Coldstream Bridge. During a dour fight the fish swam through the arch into the beat below, the line in danger of cutting on the rough stones. With great skill he steered it back until it slid on its side to Kevin, who had the net, when the split ring holding the hook to the spinner broke. The fish lay for a moment and then wavered off into the peaty water, gone forever. DW did not sleep for three nights; Kevin would not sleep for a week for he takes such things badly and, what was more, it was his spinner. The sea trout and couple of brownies they did land were cold comfort.

Two good salmon (one lost) and a sea trout in May in tricky water were not bad going, and next day the water was fining down and falling but there was a vicious wind and all morning it rained heavily, too rough for the fly unless you wanted a heavy salmon fly in your ear. We fished it hard from boat and bank and not a pull but such is salmon fishing; you have to be self-motivating and keep going, keep the bait in the water, keep at it for no fish are caught when you are sitting in the hut bemoaning the weather. The fly to catch most fish is the one longest in the water. Unlike trout fishing there is little mileage in changing methods. A salmon will not take now, but five minutes later he will; his lie is empty all morning and at midday a fresh fish comes off the tide to occupy it. Such are the charms of the game.

● ● ●

D AY THREE WAS DRY AND THE RIVER STEADY. For the first hour the wind eased for long enough for me to get back up the Duddo with the fly. I chose a Temple Dog tied by Number Two son Peter in the United States. Brendan had little faith in it but our other choices had done nothing for two days so this could do no worse. Short line at first, cover the close water, then pull off a yard or two and search further out. After half an hour I was long casting, the fly swinging through the choppy water behind the boat when almost round to 'the hang' the line twitched, a dead leaf or a twig perhaps. 'That's him...', said Brendan as though he had been waiting at home for an important visitor and suddenly there was the knock at the door. A salmon is always 'him' or 'he' as in, 'He often lies behind yon rock.'

A fifteen foot rod and as many stones of yours truly went into action, the Hardy reel sang like a corncrake and a heavy fish bored away. Given extra weight by the powerful current we followed in the boat to save line. With the backing splice way out he stopped and sulked, and then began to bang his head to shake out the annoyance. Next a series of short powerful runs followed by surges on the surface when he lashed at the line making the water boil with his great tail. Heart in mouth I hung on, for surely he would get off. He began to tire but the anchor would not hold in such strong water. Brendan manoeuvred us close enough to the bank to tie the mooring rope to the stub of an ash. Now we had to change places so he was downstream with the net, and just as the wobbly swap-over was half way through, the salmon set off on an unstoppable run downstream. On and on he went and I tightened the check on the Hardy until it squealed. This time I just knew he was coming off but miraculously he did not. The strain he had mocked began to tell and with shorter bursts of resistance he came in a bit at a time until, glorious moment, Brendan slid the net under his silver bulk and lifted him out.

Trembling I sank onto the thwart and gloated over his magnificence, the sea lice on his back, the way he threw back the weak sunlight with his shine, his broad flank, neat head and tail like a shovel. My other springers this year all had been returned and this was the only fish I would be taking so the priest administered the last rites and he was mine. We fished on but I had to keep turning my head to admire him where he lay in his glory on the bottom boards. It was a proud angler who marched to the hut, generous was the praise of fellow anglers and my hope was that they might be as fortunate. I gave my place in the boat to the bank angler and we flogged the day away with no more luck.

On the long way home I reflected on sporting companions, on the quiet expertise of Brendan and Kevin, on the king of fish and the privilege of being on that stunning river with oystercatchers, otters, sandpipers, mallard and warblers in the willows. I was grateful to hear the old clock on Coldstream church strike the quarters, to admire the magnificent limestone bridge, to think of ancient anglers including my hero William Scrope who had fished that river, to be grateful to Number Two son Peter for his special fly and Number One son David for his companionship. Thanks to the family for coming down at lunchtime to encourage us and thanks to the weather god who gave us a chance. Commiserations to poor DW and his lost fish, a disaster but one part of the agony and ecstasy of salmon fishing. Three salmon hooked, a sea trout landed and four brown trout was the bag, not bad for a tough time of year.

The blind man in the dark room had stumbled on his black cat but even if he had not, those were days not to be forgotten. Shooting has its magic moments but to catch a Tweed salmon at buttercup time runs it pretty damn close.

'A Great Big Enormous Trout...'

(A Tale of Jeremy Fisher by Beatrix Potter)

Trout fishing used to be the province of the tweedy set and to this day they it is who have the best of the dry-fly brown trout waters. For the rest of us it was lucky that the country felt a need for water, which meant more reservoirs, and more reservoirs of unpolluted water screamed out to be stocked with trout. They were not any old trout either for the rich, newly flooded farmland meant burgeoning insect life and rapid growth. The early 'reso' days in the mid sixties when Grafham Water opened for angling produced rainbow and brown trout into double figures with four, five and six pounders not uncommon. The 'tweedies' on the chalk streams believed that a half- pounder was the stuff of dreams and their tackle reflected it. Their angling world was of dainty split cane rods made by Mr Hardy of Alnwick and delicate reels with dressed silk lines, tiny flies invented by long dead vicars stuck into leather fly wallets, river keepers and squires – a way of fishing unchanged since The Old Queen passed away.

To try that gear on the new breed of monstrous trout, and many did, was to see it smashed, torn and sometimes dragged out of a boat never to be seen again. New tackle was needed so the lovely split cane gave way to fibre glass and then carbon fibre; silk lines were ousted by plastic and the dear old flies like Greenwell's Glory and Pale Watery Upright were kicked into touch by hooligans like the Dog Nobbler, the Boobie and Badger Matuka. Trout anglers now came from the ranks of the other ranks, some of them asylum seekers from coarse fishing. Lost were the old manners, the gentlemanly sportsmanship and the love of frail, old tackle. Some of the new boys even had trout fishing competitions where money was to be won and cheating, let it be whispered, was not unknown. Some would fish your water without a thought or word of apology, they killed and sold the fish they caught and some even wore baseball caps. Such conduct shook the old trout fishing clubs to their foundations.

It was easier to fish well with the new tackle; casting improved, there was no regular line greasing to make it float and the old days had gone. Purists still seek out the delights of Test and Itchen but even they use carbon rods and plastic lines that float all day. They pay a good deal more than the new stillwater fisherman who enjoy cheap sport. Soon every farm reservoir and duckpond was stocked with fast-growing rainbows and the sport soared to new heights of popularity. Once I was invited onto a pleasant beat on the Test belonging to American purveyors of all things fishing, Messrs Orvis. The river keeper was the delightful Major Jim Haddrell who now strolls on banks of Elysian streams leaving our world of dry-fly angling the poorer for his passing. For a stillwater man it was bliss to stand by a chalk stream where kingfishers darted, swans grazed in water crowfoot and mallard with broods of lusty ducklings sneaked beneath the overhang of the bankside vegetation. There were trout too, dimpling the surface and they could be seen through the polaroids, so unlike in the reso where 'chuck and chance it' are the tactics.

Jim selected a tiny dry fly, tied it onto a gossamer thin leader and I was on my own. Spot a trout, keep out of sight for they are not blind, lengthen line and flick the offering above it so it floated past naturally. Easier said than done for this was all new stuff. I got the hang of it in the end and caught a brace, waiting while the white mouth opened, the water swirled and the fly vanished. It is tempting for a lake trout man to strike like a cobra and pull the fly from the fish's mouth. I did this once or twice and then by an immense effort of will resisted and began to score. One good fish of about three pounds resisted my efforts. He would come and look at the fly as it drifted past, or I would carelessly allow it to drag unnaturally across the current, spooking him. I tried on and off for an hour, resting him and returning with a new fly but he was not born yesterday. He lay behind a clump of ranunculus and I could see every spot on his handsome body.

Jim sauntered past and I pointed out the fish and my dilemma. He explained patiently that the fly had to be placed precisely on the trout's nose giving him no time to assess it and make a decision to reject it. He must see it just in time, react instantly, take it and be caught. I must have looked sceptical for, taking the rod, Jim did one false cast and bringing the rod to the tip of his nose, a trick he used when he wanted to aim especially straight, he flicked out the fly. It landed inch perfect ahead of that fish's snout, the trout snatched it and was hooked. To add insult to injury Jim handed me the rod to play the fish and wandered on, no more words but a sharp lesson delivered. The angling world needs more people like Jim Haddrell.

The still waters had their magic moments too. Take the end of a roasting hot day on Grafham in the golden years. Our boat bobbed gently downwind, teams of old-fashioned wet flies trickling through the surface. Sedges and chironomids were hatching by the billion, moth-like they coated every surface on the boat, fluttered into eyes, up nostrils and down ears. The trout gorged on them. Hatching sedges move rapidly through the water ere they emerge. See a trout rise once here, next moment there, ten

169

seconds later further on and drop your fly on the spot where you think he will show next. The next five seconds are the most exciting a stillwater angler can experience. Either nothing happens for the fish has moved on or changed direction or there is a swirl, the leader twitches and he is on. Strike and it sets off as though on fire; for some reason trout hooked in that way always fight above their weight.

We took a wonderful basket of slab-sided trout in perfect condition, ideal for the table – and what sport. It was in the early days of lake trout fishing and I was using an ancient three-piece split cane rod made by the classic maker Cummins of Bishop Auckland given me by a kind man in my village. At dusk, drifting onto a lee shore, my fly was snatched by a trout in the five-pound class that roared away while I tried to hold it. After ten minutes of fireworks, close to the boat and tiring it did a sudden desperate plunge, the top ring snapped off and one by one the other rod rings pinged away from their ancient whippings. Now I was playing the best fish of my life on the butt section and two rings. Not surprisingly it got off. The Cummins was repaired and consigned to a dignified retirement. Another 'best' fish lost was in my pipe-smoking days when an enormous trout fairly caught and played out on Grafham Water was almost ready for the net. I could see its eye the size of a threepenny bit. Stretching the rod high in the air and back over my head to get the net to it, I was fishing a very long cast, the nylon brushed across the bowl of the curly pipe that in those days was permanently clamped in my jaws. There was a sizzle, the leader burned through and another fine fish faded away into the depths.

I have fly fished for fifty summers in waters far and near, from Swedish Lapland to the Amazon, wide, narrow, still and flowing. It has taken that half a century for the penny to drop and for me to realise the delight of fishing is not in the size or number of the fish caught but in the place, the weather, the tactics, the people, the joy of a well-executed cast, the animals and birds and being one with nature, things that ought to be at the heart of all field sports. Travel too quickly and competitively though life and you have no time left to smell the flowers…

The Fly at Night

A Cumbrian farmer friend of a friend owned two fields that ran down behind his stone house directly onto a small tributary of the Border Esk. Three shelving, shingle banks dipped their toes in water that chuckled and gurgled past where swallows and martins hawked and the dipper dipped. Sea trout ran it as did the odd salmon, so one dark night in high summer found three old friends marching down the meadow, rods made up and bags on backs each separating from his pals as he reached the water, taking his allotted shingle spit. We were advised to wait until pitch dark before fishing for sea trout and not be tempted to splash about in the gloaming so we lounged on soft shingle, watching the birds, smoking our pipes and reading the water. Old hands make a point of memorising the area behind where back casts might tangle in trees with the nightmare scenario of pulling, blasphemy and lost tackle.

It was almost pitch dark and I watched a barn owl hunting moth-like along the far bank when I heard a swishing from the pool above me. Dick the expert was making a start. Needing no more encouragement I took the rod, moved to the waterline and started lengthening line. Chuck it across, not too far, upstream mend and let it swing round like a miniature version of salmon fishing. This adventure was all of forty-five years ago and I do not think I have had such exciting fishing before or since.

Sea trout are soft-mouthed and I lost count of the little plucks that tweaked the line and had me striking like a marlin fisherman. Sometimes six consecutive casts would produce six rises and not one fish. A few managed to hook themselves on my small Peter Ross, the line hissing out, a sharp fight and then a silver darling brought into the shallows and drawn flapping onto the stones. Many were returned but the old hunter-gatherer took enough one pounders for a fry-up of one of the tastiest fish that swims. Hearing sharpened so that a tangle could be detected by the sound of the line as it swished back and forth. Like a blind man, other senses were accentuated and when the tell-tale change of note was heard it was time to retreat from the water, fire up the little torch and make good the damage. I had two spare casts round my hat with flies tied on in case of what Dick called, 'a nest of buggers', a tangle that no human fingers could undo. If you enjoy undoing tangles, he advised, do it at home in the kitchen and don't waste valuable fishing time.

I had the odd gloat at my five silver fishes lying on the pebbles but approached them with care. Someone told the cautionary tale of the sea trout angler who returned to his catch to find a large rat gnawing a fish's tail. He shooed it away but it bit his finger and the poor chap contracted the dreaded Weil's disease that all but did for him; he was never a well man again. The evening ended in spectacular fashion for a better fish snatched at the ragged little fly and this time it stayed on. It ripped back and forth across the pool and managed three spectacular leaps and thunderous splashes. Heart in mouth lest it get off I steered it in at last and there it lay, a silver ingot of a good two and a half pounds. That would do me. The fish were taking less often now and it was all but time to go to bed, just time for half a dozen final casts.

The evening had one more trick up its sleeve. I had promised myself just one more cast before leaving that delectable place for ever, when the rod tip went down with a bang. A monstrous fish had taken me and set off downstream as though on fire. It walloped down one little waterfall at the bottom of the pool, swattered down another in the pool after that and so on for four quite long pools until my backing was all but gone. The fish did an enormous leap and smashed down onto the cast that, well thrashed during the evening sport, broke like cotton. With trembling hand I wound in for that was definitely that as far as the fishing was concerned. The river had enjoyed the final word.

It could have been an enormous sea trout but wise old Dick was closer to the mark. 'Salmon', he said succinctly, and that is what it was. Hard to land a fish that might have weighed eight or ten pounds on a tapered sea trout cast on a rocky river in the dark but there can be few things better for an adrenaline rush and a breathtaking thrill to end a very special night. I never went back to that magic place; the other players in the drama are dead and gone but to this day I think about it for the memories are indelible and cannot be stolen from me.

Recipes

Nothing beats the thrill of catching and then cooking wild fish especially as they have a superior flavour: farmed salmon and trout compare favourably with white fish such as cod, haddock and plaice in price but they are much richer in healthy fish oils.

Ideal for entertaining, whole salmon or sea trout may be poached in a fish kettle or curved to fit in a large saucepan. Just cover with water, add a chopped onion, some herbs and seasoning, bring to the boil and simmer for 3 minutes. Then turn off the heat and leave to cool for 12 hours. Any size or piece of fish to be served cold will cook perfectly using this simple method.

To serve the fish hot, roast in the oven or bake in foil with herbs and white wine. If the fish is too large to fit into the oven on its side curve it in the swimming position fixing head to tail with string. To calculate the cooking time measure the fish around its thickest part and allow 4 minutes per 2.5 cm (1 inch). Alternatively fillet a large salmon or cut into 2.5 cm (1inch) steaks and freeze in family-size portions. A trout over 1 kg (2 pounds) is worth filleting. Invest in a pair of blunt-ended fish tweezers to remove any bones left after filleting. Feel for these by running your forefinger over the fish from the head to tail end. Small whole trout especially the wild brown are delicious grilled or fried in a little oil and butter and served with black pepper and a squeeze of lemon juice.

The late Jim Haddrell, a famous river keeper on the Test, gave me an unusual recipe for trout that has become a favourite. Lay the fish on a large square of foil that has been brushed with oil. Fill the body cavity with muscovado sugar, pour over some white wine and lemon juice and fold the foil to make a parcel. Cook in the oven or on a barbeque for 10–20 minutes depending on the size of the fish. Alternatively place in a dish instead of foil, cover with cling film and cook in the microwave, an ideal way to cook any fish as it preserves all the juices.

Hot or cold smoked salmon and trout provide a variety of starters, snacks and light lunches. Serve hot smoked salmon or trout with salad, cold smoked on oatcakes with a squeeze of lemon and black pepper or make a pâté or mousse.

Gaula Salmon

Serves 4

This recipe is named after the famous Norwegian salmon river. Dill, which is widely used in Scandinavian dishes such as gravadlax, has an aromatic, slightly aniseed flavour. Its name is derived from the old Norse *dilla* meaning to soothe or lull and was given to infants to cure hiccoughs. Its fresh leaves are used in pickled cucumbers and it combines well with mustard and lime to serve with fish. Allow one steak per person.

4 salmon steaks about 2.5 cm (1 inch) thick
Salt and black pepper
2 tbsp lime juice
1 tbsp mild mustard
1 tbsp chopped dill leaves or 4 tsp dried dill
2 tsp sugar
Fresh dill and lime wedges for garnish

Pre-heat the oven to 180°C/350°F/gas mark 4

Place the steaks in a baking dish and season with salt and pepper. Mix the lime juice, mustard, dill and sugar and pour over the steaks. Cover with foil and bake in the oven for 15 to 20 minutes. Alternatively arrange the steaks in a circle with the thinner ends towards the centre, cover and microwave for about 5 minutes per 450 g (1lb) fish. For an alfresco meal wrap each steak with a portion of the sauce in a parcel of foil and cook on the barbecue.

Garnish with sprigs of dill and lime wedges, and serve with new potatoes and asparagus.

Layered Salmon

Serves 6

This is an impressive way to serve either farmed salmon fillets or even better, a filleted grilse, which these days tend to be quite small due to a shortage of food in the wild.

Olive oil
2 x 700 g (1½ lb) salmon fillets
350 g (12 oz) peeled prawns
225 g (8 oz) cream cheese
1 tbsp chopped tarragon
Sea salt and black pepper
2 lemons

Pre-heat the oven to 180°C/350°F/gas mark 4

Brush a long shallow oven-proof serving dish with olive oil. Soften the cream cheese then mix with the peeled prawns, tarragon, salt and pepper. Place one fish fillet skin-side down in the dish and spread with the cream cheese filling. Place the second fillet skin-up on top to make a sandwich. Brush the skin with a little olive oil and sprinkle with black pepper. Roast 35 minutes.

Decorate the dish with lemon wedges and either hot French beans or lots of parsley before carving.

Salmon Cakes with Red Pepper Sauce

Serves 4

My childhood memories of fishcakes were those served for breakfast consisting of a few flakes of cod and a large amount of mashed potato left over from the previous night's supper. The best salmon cake I have ever tasted was at the 'once visited never to be forgotten' Ivy restaurant. This recipe, which is enough for four, has its origins in the Deep South of the United States where the fish is likely to be catfish or crab meat.

450 g (1 lb) cooked salmon, flaked
250 g (9 oz) bag cooked basmati rice
1 red pepper, finely chopped
1 red chilli, deseeded and finely chopped
1 large egg, beaten
1 tbsp flat leaf parsley, chopped
Zest of ½ lemon
Coarse salt and freshly ground black pepper
1 tbsp oil
Flat leaf parsley for garnish

Combine the salmon, rice, pepper, chilli, beaten egg, parsley, lemon zest, salt and pepper and shape spoonfuls of the mixture into eight cakes. Heat the oil in a pan and fry the cakes for 2 minutes on each side or until golden brown.

For the Red Pepper Sauce
2 red peppers, deseeded and chopped
4 large tomatoes, peeled and chopped
2 tbsp lemon thyme
1 tbsp tomato paste
Tabasco sauce to taste
Salt and black pepper

Combine the tomatoes and peppers in a saucepan and simmer on a low heat until they are very soft. Purée in a food processor, and stir in the tomato paste. Add the lemon thyme and season with Tabasco, salt and pepper.

Place a spoonful or two of the sauce on a plate, arrange the salmon cakes on top and garnish with parsley.

Trout in a Basket

Serves 4

Holidaymakers on the Algarve will have seen beach barbecues where locally caught sardines sizzle in flat, wire baskets. I usually wrap trout in foil before barbecuing to prevent the fish from breaking up or the skin from sticking to the grid when turning over. One of the hinged baskets that come in various shapes and sizes may solve this problem. There is even a fish-shaped one perfect for a whole fish, and another specially designed to hold sausages. The baskets may be turned over to cook the food on both sides with no fear of it falling onto the hot coals or sticking to the grill.

4 small trout
2 oranges
150 ml (¼ pt) orange juice
1 tbsp wholegrain mustard
2 tbsp runny honey
1 tbsp fresh chopped tarragon
Salt and freshly ground black pepper
Oil to grease the wire basket
Fresh tarragon for garnish

Grate the rind from one orange into a dish large enough to hold the fish. Add the orange juice, mustard, honey, tarragon, salt and pepper and mix well together. Slice the orange into rings and put one inside each fish. With a sharp knife, make diagonal slashes along each side of the trout, coat in the marinade and leave for 2 hours, turning once or twice. Remove the trout and reserve the marinade.

Grease the grill or the basket, if using one, and barbecue the fish over a medium to high heat for 5 minutes on each side until the skin is crisp. Tip the marinade into a small saucepan and heat until bubbling. Cut the second orange into wedges, drizzle the marinade over the trout and garnish with fresh tarragon and the orange wedges.

Chilli Trout

Serves 4

Fillets of trout may be poached, fried or grilled with a breadcrumb or herb and nut topping. Here they are marinated in oil, red chilli and balsamic vinegar, and then baked on a bed of potatoes, fennel and mushrooms.

After filleting the trout remove any remaining bones with fish tweezers.

1 kg (2¼ lb) trout, filleted
450 g (1 lb) potatoes, washed and thinly sliced
1 large bulb fennel
225 g (8 oz) mushrooms, sliced
Olive or rapeseed oil

For the marinade
Olive oil
1 tbsp balsamic vinegar
1 red chilli pepper, deseeded and chopped
2 tsp fresh thyme
Salt and black pepper

Pre-heat the oven to 200°C/400°F/gas mark 6

Mix together the ingredients for the marinade in a shallow dish, big enough to hold the fish. Cut each fillet in half and place flesh-side down in the marinade. Leave in the refrigerator for at least 2 hours.

Place the potato slices on a large oven tray, drizzle with oil and season with salt and pepper. Bake for 30 minutes or until brown. Boil the sliced fennel for 5 minutes and drain well. Heat some oil in a frying pan and fry the mushrooms and fennel until they start to colour, then add them to the browned potatoes mixing them together. Lay the trout fillets flesh-side down on the vegetables pour over any remaining marinade and return to the oven for 20 minutes.

Take the tray to the table and serve with a green salad.

Hannah's Roasted Sea Trout

Serves 8

Sea trout has a much denser and slightly less oily texture than salmon. This memorable fish was caught that day by my other half, and cooked the same evening by our daughter-in-law. One side was more than enough for four of us. The other side was equally good served cold the next day with salad.

2.25 kg (5 lb) sea trout
3 tbsp fresh thyme leaves
3 tbsp olive oil
Sea salt
Black pepper
Bunch fresh thyme
4 limes
4 fresh bay leaves, cut in half

Pre-heat the oven to 200°C/400°F/gas mark 7

Calculate the cooking time by allowing 4 minutes to 2.5 cm (1inch) measured round the thickest part of the fish. Mix together the thyme leaves, olive oil, sea salt and black pepper. Cut 3 to 4 slashes along the length of the fish on both sides. Rub the thyme mixture onto the sides, into the slashes and inside the body cavity together with the bunch of thyme. Cut the limes in half and trim the pointed ends. Push the cut end of a bay leaf into each lime half. Place the trout and limes on an oiled baking tray and roast for the calculated time. It is likely to be between 40–45 minutes. The skin should be crisp and the limes soft.

Serve immediately with spicy potato wedges and a green vegetable.

CHAPTER ELEVEN

Pike and Eel

The Three Pickerels

That is the name of a pub at Mepal in Cambridgeshire and what better one could there be for a riverside tavern than a trio of young pike? It crouches out of the wind on the banks of the New Bedford River and time was when it provided beds and hearty meals for coarse anglers and wildfowlers who sported on the Ouse Washes hard by. Years ago I was a regular and sat under my green umbrella out of the searing wind watching a *Fishing Gazette* pike bung bobbing on the leaden ripples. Piking in those days was a sport for the hard winter and a demanding pastime for an angler who did what he could to keep warm, flapping his arms vigorously round his body, marching up and down with his breath hanging like cigar smoke on the frosty air or in extremis making a fire of dead willow boughs from the nearest pile of flotsam. He was kitted out, no expense spared, in ex-military gear that in those post-war days was cheap, easily available and of good quality. You could get a sheepskin flying jacket for a fiver along with the best woollen long underwear, great coats, thick gloves and woolly hats. You needed it for in those days we had real winters.

Pike are almost as chancy and unpredictable as salmon and many an hour was spent gazing at the float with nothing to show for it. 'I wish I had your patience,' non-angling friends remarked. Patience? Not a bit of it. The angler is the most impatient person on God's earth for he believes that in the very next nano-second his float will shoot under to the pull of a fish of a lifetime that will make him the toast of riverside pubs throughout the length of the land. Of course it never happens but the whole point is that one day it just might. The closest I got was as a lad fishing a remote fenland drain, narrow and tranquil but they often held the largest pike. My dead bait had been taken, the float glided and then angled beneath the surface. There is something sinister and stealthy about the snaking out of line pulled by some invisible force on the other end. The timing of the strike is vital for the hard-mouthed, toothy monster will spit out your bait and your hooks too. Time it just right, say a brief prayer to Old Izaak and strike with all your might. One of two things happens: there is a sullen resistance and a throbbing power somewhere in the deeps, or more often, no resistance at all and the bait comes away and flies out of the water to land at your feet. It is hard to describe the emotions of a young lad when such a thing happens.

In this case the fish stayed on, a smallish jack pike of about four pounds just about big enough for eating – the cook avoids the big fish that are better returned to the water while the tiddlers are nothing but bones. A four or five pounder is about right. I was reeling it in, all resistance gone and was about to slide the net beneath it when there was an almighty swirl that startled me out of my wits, a massive head full of needle teeth and glaring eye broke the surface, an enormous pike clamped onto my fish and shook it like a terrier with a rat. For about four seconds a huge weight bent the rod until it seemed bound to break and then it was gone, the monster along with a fair proportion of my pickerel. Who can hazard a guess at the weight of that mighty fish, for the angler is the last person to trust given that the brethren of the riverbank are prone to exaggeration? With the hindsight of half a century I might hazard the *avoir dupois* at a good twenty-five pounds but we will never know. Had I landed such a monster it would have done my reputation as an angler no harm at all, although I would have had to kill it for proof and that was distasteful even in those days.

Another encounter with *esox* – my very first – was as a boy of nine fishing in a clear, shallow fenland drain with my old pal David. I had saved up and bought a Colorado spoon for three and sixpence (about 17p), a large silver thing with a propeller and a tag of red wool on a vicious treble hook that would have held the *Lusitania*. I did not really know how to work it but was terrified of losing it in the weeds so confined my inexpert casting to the open places. I enjoyed watching it twirling slowly across the muddy bottom; David was fishing fifty yards along the bank.

I was reflecting that I had little faith in its powers when from nowhere in a heart-stopping moment a pike flashed at it and seized it crosswise in its mouth. It was a goldfish bowl where I could see every scale on him and even the two ends of my spoon sticking out of either side of his mouth. It was a small pike of about four or five pounds but when it is your first one it seemed a giant compared to the roach I usually caught. Instead of doing what I should have done and striking mightily I froze, the pike froze and for a moment the world stood still, a scene seared into my memory. I dared not call David for he might have come running, the fish would have let go and he would not have believed me. The pike broke first and with a mighty ejection of air spat the bait out and it lay on the weeds on the bottom. Slowly I wound it in and to this day have not told David the story for to have informed him airily that a great pike had taken my bait but spat it out would have been such an obvious and transparent fib that nobody would have believed it. Poor David Robinson has since gone to a better place so he will never know the truth.

● ● ●

FLASH THE PAGES OF THE DIARY FORWARD a fair chunk of the century and we are netting my carp pond to remove the smaller fish that the big ones might wax even bigger. Coarse fish had come in as eggs and fry down the feeder pipe that runs in directly from the River Cam. There was great excitement when a pike of ten pounds was hauled in thrashing in the trammels amongst the carp and bream. I was surprised to see one that big but it had waxed fat by guzzling my precious carp fry and in a small, still water did not take too much exercise. It was a pretty, well-proportioned fish and by eating others was only obeying its instincts. Probably it was doing me a favour by keeping down the tiddlers for the big carp were too much of a mouthful for him. I took my eye off it for a few minutes to attend to another matter, turned round to examine it more closely but it had gone. 'Where's the pike?' I enquired of the netsman. 'It slipped and hit its head on the spanner,' he replied so that was that. That fish was rolled in breadcrumbs and translated into fishcakes before the sun went down.

Pike can grow to enormous size like the one they found floundering in the last muddy puddles of the vast Whittlesey Mere after they drained it while those from Irish and Scottish lochs have gone into folklore and legend. They have been reported as attacking drinking horses, toy yachts, nudists, bathers, swans, ducks, water voles and swimming dogs. They have something of the nightmare about them and piking specialists adopt a brooding demeanour like haunted men. Unlike most fish a pike can look at you with both eyes at once, it is a superbly designed predator, it eats anything and can give a careless handler a nasty nip or even a dose of the dreaded Weil's disease. As well as feeding the dreams of the lone fisherman (there is a Pike Anglers' Club of Great Britain), they are food of a more substantial and temporal nature. To their numerous special qualities you might add that they are good to eat and in olden times kept hunger from the door of many a fenman's damp hovel.

Eerie Eel and Prickly Perch

Unless you hail from Eastern Europe where any coarse fish is deemed delicious and Christmas dinner is boiled bream or carp, there are not many coarse fish that we enjoy. Pike is one, and the only others are eels and perch although the Victorians would sit down to a nice fry-up of bleak or gudgeon. The rest taste like lightly boiled mud full of pins. Even pike and perch are not much eaten now save by a few old-timers but those who turn up a nose at the prospect miss a treat, the more so since sea fish are being fished out and we ought to be looking closer to home to satisfy our needs.

Most anglers have a soft spot for perch. That bold stripy shape exuding testosterone and aggression, the appeal of the predator, the spiky dorsal fin, the bold bite and the spectacular fight are endearing. Also they are not the hardest fish in the world to catch. An early perch fishing memory is on the teal pond on Nacton Decoy in Suffolk where in winter wildfowl were taken for the market and later on ringed and released for research. Don Revett was the decoy man at the time and he allowed two fishing days a year on one of his ponds where the perch swarmed. This was to be a boy's day so I turned up with one young son on day one and his brother on day two. Don had made available to us the little open punt he used to break the ice in hard winters.

The shore was ringed with the dour and guileful Framlingham Anglers, one of
the oldest fishing clubs in the land. They were having a match so we poled out to the
middle moored by the lily pads and kept out of the way. It could not have been a better
classroom for a small boy trying to master the mysteries of a fixed-spool reel. Had he
fished from the bank the day would be spent undoing tangles, the line would have flown
into high trees or wrapped round his rod tip. In the boat, away from snags, a bad cast
mattered little for the bait just fell in the wrong part of the water and not into a thorn
bush. It took no more than half an hour for the line to be flying out in roughly the right
place and the lesson was learned, a lesson remembered by both boys to this day.

Another joy of perch fishing is that you use a satisfyingly chubby red float that bobs
cheerfully on the green ripples; none of the sneaky hi-tech, silent but deadly methods

favoured these days. What was more, you used a lively worm dug from the garden the day before and a big hook, for when a perch bit he did it as though he meant it. There was no half-hearted nibbling or cautious tasting, he went for it. The float gave a predatory bob to warn you to get ready and then shot under so you struck like a tuna fisherman with a bamboo pole. After a brief struggle the perch was hauled inboard pricking and snapping and dropped into the keep net. Those perch came from the same mould each being nine inches long and identical. No boy will ever tire of hauling in such fish and by the end of the day the keep net was bulging.

The following day I repeated the drama with the other son, so in two cracking days at Nacton Decoy we had two enormous nets of feisty perch and each of the boys learned to handle a fixed-spool reel. It was what our American cousins would call 'stacked wins'.

As for eels, generations of East Anglians were reared on their rich, fatty flesh. They were used as tithe to pay the monastery, someone in Sutton in the Fens paid eight stones of eels a year to the church. A bootlace made of eel skin kept the rheumatics away and you caught them with methods as old as the Saxons including glaive, hive, grig, fyke net and a score of others, each device made with materials found in the nearest osier bed or blacksmith's scrap heap. The man who drives the digger often brings me an eel. He does what is known hereabouts as a 'slubout' on my duck pond or a fen dyke and leaves a cryptic message, 'eel in bag hanging on willow behind your seat', and sure enough, there it is with the flies already beginning to gather. Charlie leads a lonely and sedentary life on the seat of a JCB and is not so good on his legs these days but when he spots an eel hauled out in his bucket with the liquid mud he becomes a striking cobra. He is out of that cab like a panther and a calloused hand darts out and rarely misses its squirming prey. Such an adventure brings a little sunlight into an otherwise routine and dull sort of day.

Eels have a faintly sinister air; round them tales accumulate and like all fishermen's yarns they grow. There was the mighty eel of Whittlesey Mere in Cambridgeshire left stranded in the last puddles when they drained that vast, shallow lake with a centrifugal pump called Appold's Pump displayed at the Great Exhibition in 1851. This nightmare was 'as thick as a man's leg at the widest part', and had a head 'big as an owd dawg'. The first man to stab it with a pitchfork was thrown over in the mud, another tackled it but had the leather heel of his water boot bitten through in one snap. At last it was overcome by weight of numbers but alas was never weighed.

It must have been one not quite as big that I had on my line when fishing with a great lobworm in a deep pond on a freshwater marsh in Norfolk. It was a hot summer's day but a great thunderstorm struck; the sky darkened, the heavens thundered and lightning flickered. At the height of the storm my fat float shot under and a titanic battle followed. A huge eel made my cane rod creak with alarm as it writhed on the surface: I feared having to land such a brute. How on earth would I handle it? With a sudden surge he broke my strong line and was gone. 'Let he who hunts the tiger be sure he wants to meet it,' as Chinese philosophers say. I have never since seen an eel even approaching that size.

The old fen 'Dykers', sometimes known as 'Tigers' made good livings from eel catching, each man having his traditional stretch of river or fen drain, a fishing pitch jealously guarded. They made their own traps from the willows that grew everywhere and sold the eels to a craving market. One chap made record bags to the envy of his mates. In fact he had murdered his sweetheart and, not wishing to let her go to waste, 'chopped her up small', and used her as ground bait on his eel pitch. As a result he caught some 'masterful gret owd eels...'. Another popular method was 'babbing' where worms were threaded onto worsted wool and rolled into a ball suspended from the end of a willow pole. This was lowered into the water, the eel bit into the juicy worms but its backward pointing teeth snagged on the wool. With a gentle, easy swing the 'babber' was able to lift the eel and drop it into a bucket before it fell off. There was a knack to it certainly, but it was not rocket science.

The eel has fallen on hard times for it carries a parasite that kills it and also there might be too much harvesting of the elvers, the baby eels that make the long journey from the Sargasso Sea. Eels are capable of travelling overland and prefer warm, wet nights in summer. A schoolboy at my school was night fishing on the Cam when he witnessed an army of eels creeping and slithering through the grass from the pond to the river. He was so impressed that he worked on his writing skills just to be able to record the event. His behaviour also improved.

There are many claims for eels, for they are curious beasts.

Recipes

To 'slat a pike', 'fin a chub' or 'barb a lobster' were all fourteenth century terms for carving. In the seventeenth century Izaak Newton describes a lengthy recipe for a pike of 'more than half a yard' (about 45 cm) 'stuffed with herbs, pickled oysters, anchovies and a pound' (450 g) 'of sweet butter and served with a sauce made with yet more butter, the juice of 3 or 4 oranges and cloves of garlick'. He proclaims 'This dish of meat is too good for any but anglers or very honest men.' He describes the eel as a most dainty dish adding, 'the Romans have esteemed her the Helena of their feasts', and suggests threading the eel stuffed with herbs and nutmeg onto a spit, roasting leisurely and basting with butter.

Today coarse anglers in Britain unlike those in mainland Europe rarely eat what they catch. Pike taken from clean water weighing up to about 2.3 kg (5 pounds) are the best size for eating: bake them whole, filleted or cut into steaks and cooked like other white fish with firm flesh; mix cooked flaked fish with creamy mashed potato and parsnip and plenty of fresh herbs, shape into rounds and fry in butter or bacon fat to make delicious pike cakes; make a fish pie by combining cooked pike, some smoked fish, mushrooms and hard-boiled eggs with a white sauce topped with potato, breadcrumbs or crumbled crisps.

Eel stewed in a herb sauce was a popular fourteenth century recipe while 'Collared Eel' a nineteenth century recipe had it stuffed with herbs and spices and boiled in vinegar and salted water. It was left to cool and kept in the pickling mixture. Today it is more likely to be skinned, cut into small pieces and fried in batter or breadcrumbs, jellied or smoked.

Fried Eel

Serves 3–4 slices per person

1 eel, cleaned and skinned
Flour seasoned with salt and pepper
Beaten egg
Breadcrumbs
Oil or bacon fat for frying
Lemon wedges

Dry the eel thoroughly and cut into 5 cm (2 inch) pieces. Roll each piece of eel in the seasoned flour, dip in the beaten egg and coat in the breadcrumbs. Leave in the refrigerator for 2–3 hours. Fry the eel pieces in hot oil or bacon fat until crisp and golden. Drain and serve at once with a squeeze of lemon and wholemeal bread.

Pike 'n Prawns

Serves 4

2 pike fillets, skinned and cut in half lengthways
225 g (8 oz) mushrooms, sliced and fried
225 g (8 oz) cooked prawns
3 tbsp hollandaise sauce
3 tbsp crème fraîche
Salt and pepper
Lemon wedges
Parsley

Pre-heat the oven to 180°C/350°C/gas mark 4

Mix together the prawns and mushrooms and spread over each piece of fish. Roll up the fillets, secure with a wooden cocktail stick and place in a shallow ovenproof dish. Mix the hollandaise sauce and crème fraîche and spoon over the fish. Cover with a lid or foil and bake for 35 minutes.

Decorate with lemon wedges and parsley.

Index

Note: the recipes are listed on page 192

Recipes

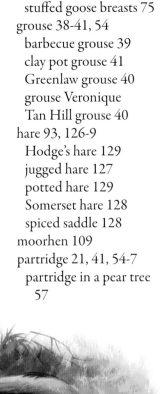